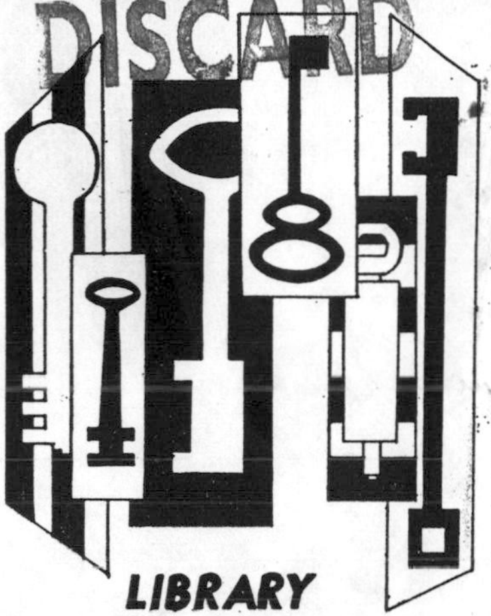

The Gesture Language of the Hindu Dance

LA MERI

The Gesture Language of the Hindu Dance

BENJAMIN BLOM, INC.

NEW YORK

Published 1964, by Benjamin Blom, Inc.,
by arrangement with the author
L.C. Catalog Card No.: 63-23185

Printed in U.S.A. by
NOBLE OFFSET PRINTERS, INC.
NEW YORK 3, N. Y.

To Johanna Jurgens, affectionately

Foreword

DANCING, as understood in India, is essentially what it was for the Greeks—not a mere spectacle, exercise, or entertainment, but "the representation, by means of gestures, of things told,"[1] a representation, that is to say, of "myths," the stories of gods and of heroes. Indian dancing is a "traditional art," and as such it has "fixed ends and ascertained means of operation." It displays a theme, not the dancer, and is the sort of art that we whose judgments of art are "aesthetic" (that is, based upon the sensations it affords us) can no longer understand.

In an individualistic culture such as ours whatever has been "handed down" is a "superstition," not merely in the proper and literal sense of the word, but in the bad sense that "survivals" date from an epoch before the "wisdom that was born with us"; because whatever we do not understand we fear or dislike. The "emancipation of the artist" and our deliberate "breaking away from tradition" in art are only special cases of our rejection of the "perennial philosophy" about which all the "traditional" arts were grouped in such a fashion as to satisfy the needs of the soul and the body together, in which sense all the arts without exception were "applied arts."

Plato held, as according to this philosophy it has been always and everywhere held, that the only things worthy of our really serious consideration are those that have to do with God. If we were able to think with him on this fundamental point, it would be as obvious to us as it was to him that we ought by every means to avoid innovation in the types of our music and dancing and that to introduce changes in the forms of art for aesthetic reasons, that is, to please ourselves or because our feelings are too much for us and must find an outlet, is nothing but a sort of slavery to our sensations. If we were such as Plato was or such as Hindus are (or were), we could agree with him in his praise of the Egyptians, "who

[1] Plato, *Laws*, 816 A.

treated all their music and all their dancing as a sacred rite," and in the view that the "laws" of art, like all other laws, are good only to the extent that they tend to make us good and are not to be judged by our tastes, which can only be trusted when they have been mastered and trained to "like" what is in itself "wholesome."

Whatever the reader may think of this theory, at any rate it accounts for the kind of art that Madame La Meri is describing; and we cannot but congratulate her upon the devoted care and real learning that have gone into the making of a book at once attractive and informative.

ANANDA K. COOMARASWAMY

Boston, Mass.
October, 1941

Acknowledgments

FOR BOTH guidance and inspiration I desire to thank most affectionately the following Indian aesthetes: my gurus, Papanasum Vadivelu Nattuvanar, of Madras, Srimati Gauri, of Madras, and Ram Dutt Misra, of Lucknow, for their long patience; G. K. Sashagiri and A. N. Kalyanasundaram, of the Renaissance Theater of Madras, for their invaluable aid; the writers K. V. Ramachandran, B.A., and V. Raghavan, B.A., (both of Madras) for the inspiration of their printed works and for their personal kindness; to K. B. Iyer, of Rangoon, for the information in his many printed articles, as well as for his personal assistance; to Dr. Ananda K. Coomaraswamy for the never-ending inspiration of his writings; to Uday Shan-kar for early inspiration and living beauty; to Professor Giuseppe Tucci, of Rome, for his help and encouragement; and to the many dancers and aesthetes in every part of India who have given me, by word of mouth the benefit of their great knowledge.

I am greatly indebted to Dr. Henry R. Zimmer for his accurate and authoritative revision of the Sanskrit terms in the text, as well as for his Introductory Chapter.

For photographs of the hand-poses, both the close-ups and the full-length shots, I must thank Guido Carreras, who took hundreds of Leica shots all over India for purposes of comparison, and who performed the difficult elimination work which eventually reduced our choice to the two hundred hastas herein given.

Acknowledgment is due the Oriental Department of the Brooklyn Museum for furnishing a photograph of the bronze of Siva Nataraja which appears on the title page.

LA MERI

New York
October, 1941

Contents

Introduction

THE RANK and dignity of the dance and the theater in Indian civilization is reflected in the pages of the Bhârata Nâṭya Sâstra. This classical treatise on the Hindu theatrical arts traces their origin back to the sacred wisdom of holy seers and priests in the dawn of Indian history. Its opening chapter describes in a mythical record how the elements of Hindu dancing sprang from the holy Four Vedas, from the revealed and inspired lore of Indian priesthood, which interprets the universe with all its divine forces and their countless manifestations through the elaborate ritual of daily worship and offerings. It was Brahmā the creator who from this fourfold Vedic wisdom, comprising hymns, melodies, prose sentences, gestures, religious procedures, and last, but not least, charms with which to win and to master the powers of nature, condensed and extracted a fifth Veda, containing the basic lore of dancing and acting.

Thus, what in the Four Vedas was meant to remain the prerogative of the initiate priest became available for the entertainment and instruction of mankind at large, regardless of caste, of sex, and of age. Hindu dance and theater constitute the exoteric world-wide counterpart of the esoteric wisdom, initiating Hindu genius into the divine forces which unceasingly evolve and maintain the universe and all its creatures.

The particular virtues of the Four Vedas became part of the secular revelation of divine reality underlying universal life. For the inspired poetry of the "Veda of Hymns" (Rig-Veda), evoking visions of the divine forces in their various personal and elementary manifestations, yielded its contents as well as its metrical patterns. From the holy meters Hindu dance acquired its rhythms. These meters, through their rhythms, were thought of as providing ordinary human words with wings. Like winged birds, by virtue of their meters, the sacred stanzas were believed capable of soaring up to the cosmic mansions of the gods and of winning a hearing. Thus dancing, songs, and recitals became imbued with the far-reaching power of the holy incantations which unlock to the priest the realm of the hidden divine powers beyond, which summon the gods to the sacred place of worship, and which conjure godly apparitions before the inner vision of the devotee.

From the second Veda, the "Wisdom of the Melodies" (Sāma-Veda), the creator drew the musical element which beguiles demons and charms gods. Like a snake charmer by means of the tones of his flute or a priest by his magic chant, the dancer casts his spell upon the audience by the melodies accompanying his gestures.

The third Veda of the Sacrificial Formulae (Yajur-Veda) contains the countless precepts which tell how every minute gesture in preparing and offering the complex sacrifice to the host of divine beings must be performed and what formulae must be pronounced at every step and gesture of the elaborate ceremony. This ritual, in which nothing is left to chance or individual variation, provided a model for the rich vocabulary of mimic gestures. From the original pattern according to which the priest conjured the superhuman powers, appeased their wrath, and won their favor came the ceremonious gravity and the solemn dignity of Hindu dancing, which has no concern whatsoever with self-expression or with sentimental improvisation. Its clockwork-like action, the smooth automatic flow of its gestures, the flawless lucidity of its classical attitudes are modeled upon the handling by the accomplished priest-sorcerer of the magic tools in the hazardous performance of his semi-divine commerce with the cosmic powers.

The fourth Veda, that of household witchcraft and occasional rites (Atharva-Veda), adds to this threefold wisdom of worship and sacrifice the complex magic of daily life. Here nature unveils to the initiate the methods of confronting and mastering animals, plants, and implements of the human household by special charms and secret devices.

The origin of dance from this fourfold tradition of ancient priesthood explains the encyclopedic character of its message. Embodying in its symbolical language the essence of the Vedas, the Hindu art of dancing unfolds and enacts the manifestation of the divine powers of the universe. It reflects the gestures and the actions of all beings, from the gods high above to the animals and flowers below, from the circling of the stars to the melodies of the winds and the murmur of the waters.

The main task assigned by the Nāṭya Śāstra to the art of dance and to the entertainments based on its language of gestures, namely, pantomime, musical comedy, show, and drama, is the expression of feelings or states of the soul (bhāva). There are in each human psyche "static" or "permanent" moods and attitudes. They form part of man's character or type, they are inherent to his sex, age, upbringing, and profession. Other emotions and passions—the "transient" ones—are aroused by all kinds of experiences and situations. All of them have their being in the sphere of the mind, that is, in the invisible realm of the "subtle stuff" which forms man's inner life. They become visible, however, and are perceived by the senses through the outward gestures of the face and the limbs, they manifest themselves through involuntary motions and outbursts and through conscious utterances and gesticulations.

The tradition of dance imparts the technique of conveying without words all kinds of feelings and emotions, the "abiding" ones and the "transient" ones, through their proper manifestations in the sphere of vision. It is the most explicit dictionary of symbolical gesture, the detailed lore of a language in which significance, lucidity, and beauty are perfectly blended.

The gestures and the steps of the dancer and actor inspire the souls of the onlooker with the feelings they portray, exactly as the singers in our operas inspire us in pouring forth the emotions of their parts along the waves of arias into the hearts of the audience. In watching the performance, the onlooker partakes of the mighty passions of gods and demons in their mythical strife. In the gestures of the dancer he watches the ever-renewed battle between the divine order and the demonic will for power. He visualizes the history of the universe through the victories and defeats of superhuman beings. He is initiated, by their visible expression, into the secret of all human emotions. He witnesses the happiness and the bereavement of lovers, their longing for each other, their happy union, their quarrels, and their reconciliations. He shares in the lofty experiences of the saint when he overcomes the temptation of the senses and achieves the serenity of perfection. He partakes of the joy of nature, thrilled by the beneficent approach of the rainy season, as he watches the dancer performing the dance of the peacock, who through its mad dance welcomes the thundering clouds while they pour down the first drops of their lifegiving essence.

The gesture language of the Hindu dance, established at an early period and surviving the ages and the crises of Indian civilization, derives its lasting impact from the immaculate clarity of its contours, from the translucent plasticity of its classical symbolism. It is, moreover, closely related to the symbolical language of fingers, of hands, and of bodily postures which forms an intrinsic part in the daily ritual of the devotee and of Yoga practice. Both are meant to evoke the visual presence of divine apparitions in the mind of the initiate and to transform his inner being, through suggestive auto-magic, into the essence of the godhead. The intrinsic kinship of the art of dance with these practices of guiding the soul towards the highest experiences of mystic religion accounts for the purity and ceremoniousness of its gesture language. The solemn beauty and gracious aloofness of Indian painting (the Ajantā caves, for example) and of the Hindu and the Buddhist idols of gods and saviors derive from their faithful adherence to this canon of mimic expression.

This gesture language mirrors the attitudes of life throughout the visible universe and the soul of man. It is imbued with the eight "flavors" or sentiments ("rasa," literally taste, sap, juice) which constitute as many different styles or moods. The "sentiment of love," or erotic passion, ranks highest in favor. The "heroic sentiment" prevails among gods and princes in scenes drawn from the heroic epics. The "atmosphere of tranquillity" emanates from saints and from the highest divinity steeped in supramundane calm. The "comical" element makes fun of fools among men and demons and delights in their discomfiture. The "pathetic sentiment," arousing compassion, the elements of "fear and terror," of "wrath" and "disgust," too, have their proper place in the dancer's performance, as they have in the kaleidoscopic course of events. Last, but not least, the "miraculous atmosphere" has its particular function in the happy ending of plays by means of the timely apparition of beneficent gods.

All these attitudes, or "flavors," have been exhibited by the highest divinity on various mythical occasions. The all-embracing, ambivalent character of the Hindu godhead, which is universal life force evolving and destroying all and everything in its turn, comprises every attitude from the loving to the wrathful, from the heroic to the comical. The art of the dance aims to reflect the whole range of attitudes by choosing the proper subject for each in turn. Its function is to be an encyclopedic initiation into the manifold mystery of life.

For the ideal dancer and actor, according to the Hindu conception, is the highest god himself, the source and motor force of universal life. In his creative or destructive aspect he is called Vishnu, or Siva, both aspects counterbalancing each other and being fundamentally manifestations of the self-same essence. As Vishnu, this cosmic master dancer is viewed as having created, through a ceremonious dance of three solemn strides, earth, space, and the vault of the firmament. By his first step he caused the surface of earth to spring into existence under the sole of his foot. Next, as he trod into the void, his uplifted foot created the space between heaven and earth. By his third stride he shaped under his heel the solid dome of heaven, the upper surface of which is called Vishnu's "step" or "foot-print."

Dancing, in India as among archaic man in general (for example, the Red Indians dancing for rain, and so forth), ranks among the most powerful means of creative magic. Through dancing Śiva creates the universe, through dancing he dissolves it again. For the Hindu mind the unceasing dynamism of the world's life process, with innumerable beings continuously streaming into existence and stars silently fading out, is nothing but the frantic dance of this divine "King of Dancers" (Naṭarāja), unwearied by the mimic display of all the eight elements or sentiments of life. The universe is the constant manifestation of this dancer's creative life force, rushing on through death and destruction, evolving countless beings, and taking them back again like so many dreamy musical gestures of his superb four arms, swaying to the solemn rhythm of his feet, on which bells tinkle, beating the time of the world's ages.

Or this dance of the universe, whose transient gestures we, all of us, are— we as well as the slowly crumbling mountains or islands surging from the depths of the ocean—is visualized as the dance of "Śakti," Śiva's divine energy, manifesting itself as his wanton mistress, madly dancing with disheveled locks. She is the mother of the universe and at the same time is Kālī, the "Dark Lady" of the Hindu pantheon, devouring the flesh of all the creatures she has brought forth and has nourished at her breasts. All figures impersonated by the Hindu dancer, gods and men alike, are manifestations of her eternal essence: Krishna, the charming boy-savior, conquering snakes and monsters, playing the flute, and leading the dance of the maidens in the moonlit woods of the bucolic idyl of his youth, and also the innocent girl, watering the flowers in the hermitage of the saint whom she serves or warding off the obtrusive bee which mistakes her dark eye for the expanded calix of a violet lotus blossom. The play of the insect diving into the blossom in search of honey mirrors the kiss of lovers and their melting into each other. The dancer who enacts both attitudes according to the rules of the Nāṭya Śāstra discloses the secret of the highest goddess, who, being life force eternal, inspires lovers and sends the bees out on their way.

The gesture language of the Hindu dance constitutes the finest and the most elaborate tradition of dancing that has come down to us. With its almost infinite variety of expression, it affords the richest pictorial vocabulary for acting and pantomime, and in addition to its formal beauty it conveys through its symbolical attitudes the deepest thoughts of the Hindu genius. Its message should prove inspiring to the stage, as well as to the painting and the sculpture of our time.

La Meri, through a prolonged study with the local schools still hidden away in India, impersonates the most authentic tradition of the Hindu dance. By her acting and teaching she is exceptionally qualified to transmit one of the most precious lessons Old India has treasured up for modern civilization.

HENRY R. ZIMMER

New York
July 16, 1941

The Gesture Language of the Hindu Dance

Hindu Nāṭya

INDIAN Nāṭya is the most complete dance-form existing today. It is the expression in lyric movement of an inspirational, philosophic religion. Its birth is beyond the portals of time, and it is ageless. It is probable that all forms of dance-art are outgrowths of it. After many years of studying this complicated Veda, I came to the conclusion that the West needs to know and understand this visual philosophy, which is based on calmness of spirit and which is almost entirely unknown outside the borders of its own land. Moreover, the dance-expressions of the Peninsula are strange to the gurus[1] of North India. That the art is so little known to westerners, even those who travel and live in India, is probably due to the numerous regional forms of Bharata Nāṭya now existing. The stranger, beginning at the end instead of at the beginning, thinks to understand the art by seeing performances of it; and when he has seen two or three, apparently distinctly different, he becomes confused and abandons the whole idea. It is for this reason that I, who am an ardent admirer of all racial dance-expressions, and perforce especially of Hindu Nāṭya, came to the conclusion that the best way to introduce this art to the alien is to present and to explain its most outstanding technical characteristic, hastâbhinaya, and its several best-known and most typical forms. I have selected the Kathakali form, which is the great dance-drama of South India, the tāṇḍava dance of men. I have selected the Sadir Nautch of South India, the lāsya dance which inspired the bas-reliefs of Chidambaram. I have selected the Kāthak dance of North India, with its strong Mohammedan influence. These three and their derivatives have produced the modern dance-art of India, the reborn Hindu dance best exemplified in the art of Uday Shan-kar. This art, fruit of the Indian artistic renaissance, can scarcely be appreciated at its true value until the watcher knows something of the technical, the philosophic, and the classic theories upon which it is based.

[1] **For meaning of Sanskrit words see Glossary.**

It is to aid this appreciation, to help forge a key to open the door to a new beauty that delights the eye and strengthens the spirit, that I offer this book, which endeavors to set forth enough of the vast gesture-language of Indian Nāṭya to make its usage comprehensible to the western layman.

In briefly reviewing the religious background and the legendary and actual beginnings of Nāṭya, I have been motivated by the conviction that without some slight knowledge of these two it is impossible even to touch the shadow of rasa-realization, which is the main scope of Indian dancing. One must, at least, have broken the surface of this deep, still philosophy to understand the underlying meaning of conversations which occur in the Ramayaṇa between Vishnu in his avatar of Rama and Vishnu in his partial incarnation of Lakshman, or to feel the spiritual heightening brought by the immortal Bhagavad Gītā, those words which Krishna spoke to the compassionate Arjun on the field of battle.

> Thou dost feel pity where pity has no place. Wise men feel no pity either for what dies or for what lives. There was never a time when I and thou were not in existence, and all these princes, too. Nor will the day ever come in future when all of us shall not exist. . . . There is no existence for nothingness, there is no destruction for that which is. Know that the very tissue of this universe is the Imperishable; it lies in no man's power to destroy it. Bodies come to an end, but the soul which is clothed in them is eternal, indestructible, and infinite. Fight then, O Bhārata! It is as much a mistake to believe that one man kills another as that another is killed. There is never any birth nor any death. Nobody has begun, and nobody will cease to be. Having no beginning and no end, the one and only Soul is not smitten when it is struck . . . That which is born is sure to die, and that which is dead is sure to be born. Faced with the inevitable, pity has no longer any place. The origin of things escapes us; the object of our perceptions in the course of their career, they elude us once more in the end. Of what use are lamentations? Consider that pleasure or pain, wealth or poverty, victory or defeat are of equal worth. Prepare then for combat! Give thought to nothing but the act, never to its fruits, and let not thyself be seduced by inaction. For him who achieves inward detachment, neither good nor evil exists any longer here below.

The westerner who views the oriental dance must keep in mind that the dance-arts of the Orient and those of the Occident are sharply divided and that there are many contradictory points between these two, both technically and spiritually. It may be well to mention some of the more salient of these:[2]

(a) The occidental dances from the waist down; the oriental from the waist up.
(b) Occidental feet are shod, capable, point downward, and are inexpressive

[2] Flamenco and Hawaiian dances are of eastern origin and fall choreographically under that head.

in themselves: oriental feet are naked, move simply, point upward, and are expressive in themselves.

(c) Occidental technique is built on broad lines; oriental, on infinite shadings.

(d) The occidental swings the entire body to a harmonizing balance; every separate part of the oriental body has a life, a line, a rhythm of its own.

(e) The occidental curves the fingers inward; the oriental curves them outward.

(f) The occidental dance is eccentric, all movement going outward from the motive force; the oriental dance is concentric, movement curving inward about the motive center.

(g) The occidental when dancing is emotionally expressive; the oriental, dancing, compressive.

(h) Most occidental dances have courtship as the motive; most oriental dances were born in the temple.

(i) The occidental dance aims to excite; the oriental dance, to sooth.

(j) Choreography in the Occident is built like the drama, with a fast crescendo to a brillant and exciting climax; in the Orient choreography seeks to maintain an emotional level which increases only in intensity.[3]

(k) The occidental strives always to "get over" the footlights; the oriental drops an invisible curtain at the edge of the platform.

(l) In the Occident novelty, creation, originality are much prized; in the Orient perfection is based on conformation and rigid adherence to ancient rules.

(m) In the Occident the dance is a vehicle for reflecting the dancer's personality; in the Orient the dancers supresses his personality to become the vehicle of the theme.

(n) In the Occident all facial expressions and, in some forms of dance, the movement of the upper body are spontaneous in the performer; in the Orient every part of the body, as well as the facial expression, moves according to rigid laws.

(o) The occidental dancer is expected to move the emotions of his audience from the dead stop of skepticism; members of an oriental audience are

[3] It might be interesting here to compare Dr. R. K. Yajnik's outline of Sanskrit drama with Bliss Perry's of the western drama. Yajnik: Opening, Progression, Development, Pause, Conclusion. Bliss Perry: Introduction, Inciting Force of Moment, Development, Climax, Denouement, Final Suspense, Final Allotment.

Here one sees immediately the antipodal strivings of the East and West. The East seeks calm and spiritual quiet; the West, excitement and spiritual stimulation.

"content to perfect the song in their own minds, by the force of their own feelings."[4]

(p) The occidental dancer builds up to his *tour de force*, points it so that its physical difficulty is seen and understood; the ideal of the oriental is "art hidden by its own perfection."[5]

RELIGIOUS BACKGROUND

In approaching the Indian dance one must hold in mind that its *raison d'être* is purely religious. All its aspects, from the street dance, in which the folk celebrate a holy festival, to the dance-drama, in which the actor portrays incidents from the lives of the gods, stem from worship. For this reason it is singularly austere in form and pure in expression.

It is said that pure dance exists, but that there is no pure abhinaya, for abhinaya must always be rhythmic. So it is that religion may exist without dance: but dance cannot exist without religion.

Nāṭya was made from the holy Vedic books. It is a synthesis of holy liturgy. For the Vedic books are five: the Rig Veda is the book of hymns; the Sāma Veda that of songs; the Yajur Veda the formula of liturgy; the Artharva Veda, the book of incantations. And from these five Brahma created the Nāṭya Veda.

The secondary purpose of the Nāṭya Veda is to teach, but its primary aim is to evoke in the spectator the fountain of rasa, enjoyment of which has been compared to Brahmānanda.[6] And Brahmānanda is the bliss of oneness with God.

Now, Visvanatha tells us that the tasting of rasa is enjoyed "only by those who are competent thereto": and Dharmadatta says that "those devoid of imagination in the theater are but as the woodwork, the walls, and the stones.[7] The Hindu theory is that the art of art is to excite the imagination of the spectator to the emotion of imagined beauty. You yourself are the mirror. If your mind is silver-clear, then beauty is reflected therein; but dust on the mirror obscures the soul of the reflection and leaves only the muddied outlines. As care clears the surface of the mirror, so culture clears the surface of the mind. The joy of rasa-realization is potential in every man. Beauty does not exist outside ourselves. It is not a tangible thing, but an emotion which we create within us. Just

[4] Rabindranath Tagore, quoted in A. K. Coomaraswamy's *Dance of Siva* (New York, 1924), p. 34.
[5] Japanese maxim.
[6] Raghavan, "The Indian Theater," in *Sound and Shadow* (Madras, 1934), Vol. III, No. 3.
[7] A. K. Coomaraswamy, "Theory of Beauty," in *Dance of Siva* (New York, 1924), p. 33.

as happiness is a state of one's own making, so is beauty. If you admire a beautiful woman, it is not she who possesses the beauty—it is yourself. This is rasa-realization—and one step beyond it lies Sahaja, that philosophy which teaches its followers to divorce the admiration of beauty from the desire for possession.

Now since the scope of the Indian theater is the achievement of rasa-realization and since the spectator can achieve this only by the exercising of his own imagination, the theater employs a special technique to make itself rasavant. The word "dharma" means "righteousness" or "right conduct," and there are two modes of right conduct in the theater: Nāṭyadharma and Lokadharma. Nāṭyadharma is imaginative transfiguration, stylized action, stage ways. Lokadharma is imitative realism, natural action, world ways. For a simple play Lokadharma is used, as for example, an actor desiring to portray weeping does so with real tears (a form of sāttvika abhinaya). For a dance drama, Nāṭyadharma is used—to weep the dancer wipes imaginary tears from his cheeks with the tripatāka hand. "Dancing conditions everything from the simplest courtesy to the most elaborate ritual, and this helps to recapture the epic atmosphere of the stories."[8] So it becomes increasingly apparent that the watcher of Nāṭya must be something far beyond the casual spectator of the western theater. In the Nāṭya Sāstra, Bharata writes,

> The Audience shines like the Wishing-tree when the Vedas are its branches, scriptures of art and science its flowers and learned men the bees; where men of truth are found shining in good conduct, beloved of kings, adorned by the Vedas; where the Vedānta is expounded; when distinguished by the voice and lute; possessing heroes of renown, ornamented by resplendent princes, shining in royal splendor.[9]

For the audience is half the performance of any art. It is the receiving-set without which the melody is lost in the void. It is not always the artist who broadcasts the static your set sometimes picks up!

The theory of Nāṭyadharma itself presupposes philosophic culture in the spectator. To achieve rasa-realization the spectator must have not only technical knowledge, but must be steeped in the philosophic principles which govern Indian life. He must know that those gods who stride Bharata's stage are only personifications of the laws of life—that Hinduism does not concern itself with dogma, but with religion, that all its thousand gods are one god, and that god is the

[8] Ramachandran, "Dance Traditions of South India," in *Triveni* (Madras, 1935), Vol. III, p. 4.
[9] A. K. Coomaraswamy, *The Mirror of Gesture* (New York, 1936), p. 32.

Cosmic Energy. The dance-dramas of India are passion plays, and their ultimate message is deeper and broader than words can describe.

Yet there again the drama must be enacted on the Chidambaram of the heart of him who watches. To some these plays are heathenism; to some they are pretty legends; but to some they teach the Truth of the Omnipotence, the Divine Rightness of the Moving Force of the Universe; and to others they bring the rasa-realization, which is that rare moment of knowing an existence outside time and space. The Hindu gods were never meant to be taken literally. Each and every one is an attribute of the Divine Plan.

In the beginning the Vedic deities were much like those of the Greeks in that they were personifications of natural forces. Ushas was the goddess of the dawn; Sūrya, of the sun; Rātri, of the night; while Varuṇa and Indra, like Jove, were kings of heaven. Then Brahmānism and the name Brahmā came into being. Brahmā is a vague, an abstract god. He is the Creator who creates all things, who gathered into himself the opposing religions of Vaishṇavism[10] and Śaivism; who brought with him transmigration and the shadow of monism. The Trimūrti of three gods (Brahmā, Vishṇu, and Śiva) in one includes all the aspects and avatārs of each, as well as all the goddesses, who are merely feminine, or gentler aspects of their respective spouses. Pārvatī, goddess of the earth, is the śakti, or Energy of Śiva, projected outside himself in a feminine form, so that in union she will be even more a part of him. Pārvatī has many aspects: Kālī, the Black; Durgā, the Inaccessible; Umā, the Mother; Gaurī, the Brilliant; and a host of others. And all of them are aspects of the One God.

Śiva, symbol of the cosmic force, the generative force, has absorbed the Vedic gods of the whirlwind and the rain, Rudra and the Maruts. Rain, indeed, is life to India. But Śiva has many aspects besides the generative one. The principal aspects are: anugrahamūrti (beneficent); samhāramūrti (destructive); bhikshaṭanamūrti (the mendicant); nṛtamūrti (Lord of Dancers); maheśamūrti (the three-headed). Of these the most beloved are samhāramūrti, and nṛtamūrti —and the latter in the role of the Tāṇḍava Dance on the burning-ground.

The destructive deities of India destroy only evil—they destroy Māyā (illusion) and the fetters that bind the world. Their destruction is kind and pitying; it is not final, but only the crucible for the change to utter purity. Śiva dances to free the world. With his dance he destroys time and space and evil and good. And the naṭa (dancer) dances outside time and space and while she dances

[10] Included the cults of Kṛishṇa and Rāma by making these two heroes avatārs of Vishṇu.

is conscious of neither good nor evil. There is no time in Nāṭya. Like the philosophy of Nietzsche, Hinduism transcends both good and evil. It is superior to humanity, for it knows complete acquiescence. Materialism is neither good nor bad. Action and the universal dance are joyful, whatever they bring; life is an art, to the beautiful realization of which all arts and branches of learning contribute; we help God's work by joyfully and voluntarily doing our own, each well-accomplished task is a flower laid on His altar.[11] God is within us, and we are one with Him. So the Bhāgavata Purāṇa and the Gītā Govinda, recounting the loves of Kṛishṇa, when as a cowherd he played his flute on the fields of Brindaban for the delight of the gopīs, are lyric hymns to the everlasting love of God. They must never be imagined as the erotic love poems which they might appear to the casual reader to be. Theirs is a strange and tender mysticism, and if we are unable to see their spirituality, the fault lies within ourselves.

LEGENDARY HISTORY

Indian legend describes in rich detail the divine birth of the dance. The dance was the beginning of all things. Bhavānī, dancing in joy, saw come from her breasts three eggs, and from these three eggs came forth the three gods: Brahmā the Creator, Vishṇu the Preserver, and Siva the Destroyer. This holy triumvirate, born through the dance, used the dance to create the universe and all that is in it.

> In the night of Brahmā nature is inert and cannot dance until Śiva wills it: he rises from his rapture and sends through inert matter pulsing waves of awakening sound; and lo! matter also dances, appearing as a glory 'round about him. Dancing, he sustains its manifold phenomena. In the fullness of time, still dancing, he destroys all names and forms by fire and gives new rest.[12]

Of the many aspects of the god Siva, the most beloved is Naṭarāja, Lord of Dancers. The works of Naṭarāja, accomplished through the dance, are five: creation, preservation, destruction, illusion, and salvation; and the significance of his dance is threefold: "first, it is the image of his rhythmic play as the source of all movement within the cosmos; secondly, the purpose of his dance is to release the countless souls of men from the snare of illusion; thirdly, the place of the dance, Chidambaram, is in the heart."[13]

[11] Karma-yoga.

[12] A. K. Coomaraswamy, *The Dance of Siva* (New York, 1924), p. 66.

[13] *Ibid.*, p. 65.

Now Śiva, being beyond the realm of purposes and restrictions, his dance springing from the depths of his own being, his gestures were svabhāva-ja, or spontaneous, and therefore purposeless. The rules or scriptures of the Hindu dance were framed by Brahmā, the Creator.

At the very beginning of the last aeon before the present one, Indra and the other devas came one day to Brahmā and said: "We desire a pastime to be seen and heard. This matter of the Four Vedas should not be heard by Śūdras; pray, therefore, shape another and a Fifth Veda for all the castes!"

Brahmā agreed and sending away the devas, sat awhile in meditation. At last, recalling all the vedas, he drew from each a part and made therewith the Fifth Veda; from the Rig Veda he drew the words; from the Sāma Veda, the singing; from the Yajur Veda, gesture; and from the Atharva Veda, rasa.[14]

In the beginning Brahmā gave the Nāṭya Veda to Bharata. Bharata, together with groups of Gandharvas and Apsarasas, performed Nāṭya, nṛtya and nṛtta before Śiva. Then Śiva, having remembered his own majestic performance (dance) caused Bharata to be instructed in that (art) by his attendants (gaṇas). And before this, on account of his love (to Bharata) he gave to the latter instruction in lāsya through Pārvatī. Knowing about tāṇḍava from Taṇḍu, sages spoke it to mortals. Pārvatī, on the other hand instructed Uṣā the daughter of Bāṇa, in lāsya. The latter taught (the art) to the milk-maids of Dvārakā, and they taught this to women of Saurāṣṭra who (in their turn) taught it to women of other countries. In this manner this (art) was traditionally handed down and has come to stay in the world.[15]

This is the legendary beginning of the dance. Its actual birth is, as racial expressions always are, shrouded in the mists of antiquity. Even the actual period when it first took classical form seems doubtful. But on one thing all are agreed, that Bharata was the scholar who incorporated into clear rules the already existing principles of the Indian dance. Bharata's book, "the Nāṭya Śāstra, is a monumental work dealing with drama, music, aesthetics, rhetoric, grammar, and allied subjects, as well as dancing. This masterpiece of dramaturgy is divided into thirty-six chapters."[16] Now the point which arises is: What is the date of the actual birth of the Indian dance-art? Bharata's Nāṭya Śāstra seems to belong to the post-epic age. Abhinava Gupta, who lived at the beginning of the eleventh century, speaks of the Nāṭya Śāstra. But Bharata, in his famous work, refers often to others who have written on the same subject. Another

---

[14] A. K. Coomaraswamy, *The Mirror of Gesture* (New York, 1924), p. 16.
[15] M. Ghosh, *Abhinaya-Darpana* (Calcutta, 1934), Part 4, p. 2.
[16] B. V. and P. S. Naidu, *Tandava Laksanam* (Madras, 1936), p. 4.

very peculiar difficulty arises out of the fact that the name Bharata had become a common noun even before the time of the Nāṭya Śāstra. Probably the author of our work came to be called Bharata on account of his mastery of Nāṭya. Vedānta Dēsikar, the great Vaishṇavite philosopher, in his Saṇkalpa Sūryodaya, suggests that the word Bharata might be an acrostic of the initial syllables of the words Bhāva (Idea), Rāga (Tune) and Tāla (Timing). The implication seems to be that the name Bharata is merely a concept of the highest degree of abstraction symbolizing the dance with all its accompaniments.[17]

It is known that Nāṭya was practiced in B.C. 140, though it is impossible to judge how complete an art it was at that time. Certainly the naṭa sūtras were in popular usage before the writing of the Nāṭya Śāstra. Many claim that the Nāṭya Śāstra itself is a sūtra. But whatever the date of the writing of the Nāṭya Śāstra, we have conclusive proof on the walls of the incomparable Temple of Naṭarāja at Chidambaram that dancing in the formal style now known as Bharata Nāṭya existed in the sixth century A.D. Many claim that its origin goes back 6,000 years. And I am sure it does, for the origin of every formal dance is the folk dance, which originates with the first step of the first man of that race.

CHARACTERISTIC SCHOOLS

Kathakali

India is not one country, but many countries. Even as Europe presents many different forms of folk dance, each one closely or frailly linked with its neighbors, so do the various lands of India present various schools or aspects of dancing, many of them linked together only by legendary content and artistic idealism. The comparatively peaceful history of the Deccan made it possible for the arts to develop with greater purity and system in the South. For the same reason many artists, scholars, and composers settled in this section under the patronage of the Vijayanagar kings and contributed richly to artistic development. The discussion as to which of the forms of Southern Nāṭya was the original and which today is most pure is loud and unending among Indian aesthetes. Each province says, as the Upanishadic seer said of the Brahman, "It alone existed at first, naught else winked!"

The home of Kathakali is in Malabar, which lies between the Eastern Ghats and the Arabian Sea. The geographical position alone helped greatly to keep the local art from confusing outside influences. Its enthusiasts claim it has been in existence in its present form for 1,000 years or more.

[17] B. V. and P. S. Naidu, *Tandava Laksanam* (Madras, 1936), p. 4.

The basis of all Indian Nāṭya is the Mantram, or mimed chant. In Malabar this ancient chant has grown into the form of a mimed drama. The subject-matter is taken from the two great Indian epic poems, the Rāmāyaṇa and the Mahābhārata, and stories of Saivic interest. These tales the artist tells through hastâbhinaya (hand pantomime) and mukhaja (facial pantomime). "While the movement of the hand traces out an idea, the appropriate emotion is expressed through the face and eyes," and thus an entire story is told. "The dances which accompany and follow the action are many and varied." They are mostly in the tāṇḍava or vigorous style. The musical accompaniment is composed of two drums, a gong, and cymbals. During the dramatic action voices chant the story enacted; for the incidental dances a flute often carries the rāga. This primitive music is well suited to the Kathakali performance, which is of elemental vitality and is performed in the open air. Seemingly limited, this orchestra is capable of the most ear-splitting noise. Elsewhere in India the drums are played with the bare hands and fingers, but in Malabar hard finger-tip coverings make the hours of *forte* playing possible.

The outstanding characteristic of the Kathakali technique is the exaggerated control of the facial muscles and its application to the stylized expression of the different rasas (moods). The rasas have been gathered, by Bharata, under nine headings: Sṛiṅgāra (passionate), Vīra (heroic), Karuṇa (compassionate), Adbhuta (amazement), Hāsya (laughter), Bhaya (fear), Bībhatsa (loathing), Raudra (fury), Sānta (peace). Every muscle of the face is brought into play to describe these mental states and their various shadings. The brows play a very important part while the mouth has a special style of expression. The eyes roll, the nose twitches, the cheeks and the chin vibrate. Some extremely talented players, who have brought an advanced state of yoga to their art, are capable of enlarging and contracting the pupils of their eyes at will. Add to this fantastic facial technique the many fluid hastas, which are also highly developed, and the emotional control of the chest[18] (one can hear the breathing of anger far away from the stage), and the effect of the drama is highly hypnotic. The story of the drama as it unfolds is chanted by the members of the orchestra. The mute actors render this sung-tale in stylized pantomime.

Women actors are taboo on the Kathakali stage. The practice, in addition to being in conformity with the medieval Indian tradition, recognizes the fact that the extreme

[18] Vaksa Rechaka.

complexity of the Kathakali technique, which displays masculine and rather elemental vigor, is unsuited to the delicate and tender feminine frame.[19]

The women characters are impersonated very realistically by young male naṭas.

The dances of Kathakali bear the same relation to the drama itself as the ballet bears to opera; they precede a scene for the sake of indicating the mood to follow. This is particularly necessary in the oriental theater, as neither scenery nor properties are used. If we are about to witness a hunting scene, the introductory dance might be the Tiger Dance. If we are about to see a love scene in a garden, the sensual Peacock Dance might precede it. Or if two heroes engage in mortal combat, they may do so in a duet-dance. The gestures of these dances are descriptive rather than pantomimic, and as such they may be enjoyed even by those who are unacquainted with the complete vocabulary of Nāṭya pantomime. At the same time, the style and technique of the incidental dances[20] are identical with that of the dramatic action.

The procedure of Kathakali is as follows: First is the opening by the loud beating of drums, called the kelikottu; then comes the todyam, or warming-up dance (this is sometimes performed off-stage); two or more young men then enter and perform an incidental dance of a lyric style (sukumāra); then the hero is presented (purupaddu); and a musical number (melapaddu) is then played. This much is the overture to the drama. Then the play itself begins. The musicians chant the story while the actors render it in Nāṭyadharma abhinaya. Between the dramatic scenes are presented the kalasams.

"Kathakali is an all-night function, enacted on bare bround without any scenic background. A giant brass lamp filled with cocoanut oil is all the stage lighting." The musicians stand behind a curtain which is held by two men at the back of the dancing space. "A Kathakali performer is so well-trained to regard his art as the practice of yoga" that he seldom loses his hypnotic hold on the watchers. From a relatively quiet beginning, the drama mounts steadily and strongly through thirty-six hours of action to a climatic finale.[21]

Sadir Nautch

Kathakali is the most typical and finished of the dance-dramas of South India, and, as has been previously noted, is performed exclusively by men. Let

[19] All quotations on Kathakali are from K. B. Iyer, "Kathakali, Classic Dance-Drama of Malabar," *Illustrated London News* (March 20, 1937), p. 482.

[20] Kalasam.

[21] Hastas characteristic of Kathakali can be found in figures 2, 5, 9, 11, 29, 32, 33, 35, 39, 42, 49, 67, 70, 93, 96, 97, 98, 101, 131, 143, 166.

us pass now to another ancient dance-form in the Peninsula, and one practiced exclusively by women. This is called Bharata Nāṭyam or Sadir Nautch. The title leads to confusion in our minds, for we know that sometimes all Indian dancing is called Bharata Nāṭya. Yet the very fact that this dance-type is titled thus gives a certain proof to the contention of Madrasi aesthetes that this, and this only, is the dance of which Bharata wrote, all others being only offshoots of it. Tāṇḍava karaṇas were created by Siva, and their hastas are dynamic and dramatic. Bharata Nāṭyam, the lāsya dance, was created by Pārvatī, and its hastas are passionate and lyrical. Bharata Nātyam includes nṛtta (pure dance), nṛtya (expository dance), and Nautch (combination of song and gesture-dance).

It was the original dance of the courtesan-danseuse, who has been immortalized not only in the Rig Vedic hymns but in the bas-reliefs of the most beautiful of the Hindu temples, the Ajanta Caves—Bṛhadīswara Temple at Tanjore, Belur, Halebid, Mount Abu, and Chidambaram. All these show an infinite variety of typical poses. The oldest thing existing in Chidambaram Temple is a porch of fifty-six pillars eight feet high and ornamented with dancing figures which are the most perfect in South India. It is the Nṛtta or Nṛtya Sabhā—the Hall of the Dance. There are 108 of the karaṇas (dance combinations) described by Bharata sculptured in the great gōpurams of Chidambaram Temple. One has only to study these figures to know the ideal body-lines of the Southern Bharata Nāṭya.

One hundred years ago Vadivelu, dance master in a long line of hereditary dance masters, edited the performances of Bharata Nāṭyam in their present form. The selection of the items of nṛtta and abhinaya was doubtless due somewhat to the taste of the last kings of Tanjore who protected the art and its protagonists. The classical evening program lasts from three to four hours, the dancer or dancers never leaving the stage during that time and the noise of the accompanying music never ceasing, for between number and number, while the dancers rest on their feet and wipe their streaming faces, the drone wails on, and the supple fingers of the tabla-player tap his instrument gently.

All programs open with an invocational dance called "Alarippu." This was originally presented only to Siva in his own temple. In it all those muscles necessary to the performance of Sadir Nautch are "warmed up," one at a time. Many think it the most beautiful and captivating of all Nautch compositions.

The second item of nṛtta is the Jatīswara. More moved than the Alarippu, it depends mostly on the technique of the feet and legs, but is embroidered with graceful hastas and addiyams.

Tillana is the third and last item of pure dance. It is most delightful, "not at all sensuous, but infinitely aesthetic in the pantomime of maidenly capriciousness."[22]

At least ten gesture-songs are presented on a program. These include Slokas, Javalis, Varnams, Padams, and similar songs. The dances are nṛtta—or compositions of aesthetic beauty without specific meaning in the hastas. The Nautch is nṛtya—decorated with nṛrta passages. The dancer may sing the song herself, or she may have a member of the orchestra sing it. The Hindu song is simple in lyric, and each phrase is repeated several times in a variety of cadenzas. It is the art of the dancer to express through abhinaya, the phrases of the song in divers ways. For example, the singer sings: "I called my love, and he did not answer." The first time the pantomime is of the simplest—I (Fig. 174) call (Fig. 133). Listen (Fig. 132) nothing (Fig. 57, vyāvṛtta). The singer repeats: "I called my love and he did not answer." This time the dancer pantomimes: "I wrote a love message and tied it to the neck of a dove, but my love shot the poor bird, alas!" The singer repeats the phrase, "I called my love, and he did not answer." This time the dancer injects a bit of delicate humor and pantomimes: "My love stood there indifferently, so I said 'Will you come? or shall I give you a slap?'" This is the art of the Sadir Nautch, to find the loveliest and most original ways of translating the simple, singing phrases into a diversity of charming movements. During the musical interludes or cadenzas the dancer executes pure dance steps as embroidery to the song.

Certain of the more typical movements of this form of dance are the addiyams (or grīvā rechaka) of the neck, the motiṭam sthānaka (or upavishṭasthāna), sampada with anjali of the hands (see Fig. 170). The body is rigidly straight and slightly thrown forward, the hands move legato in the pantomimic passages, and generally staccato in the nṛtta passages. The facial expression follows the rules of Bharata, but in a far more moderate form that in the Kathakali school. The thattadavu (floor contacts) are often based on the doubling of the tempo, the design, translated into Western musical parlance, being: sixteen bars of whole notes; sixteen bars of half notes; sixteen bars of quarter notes; sixteen bars of eighth notes.

There is, of course, no stage setting, and the musicians (drone, tablas, singer, and the guru himself) stand across the back of the stage in the way prescribed by Bharata. There is no applause from the audience, except for some difficult

[22] K. V. Ramachandran, "South Indian Dance," in *Triveni* (Jan.–Feb., 1935), Vol. III, Nos. 4, 5.

feat, and this spatters out in the middle of the numbers. If a certain cadenza has pleased particularly, the guru may tell the dancer to repeat it.[23]

Kathak

It has been pointed out that India is not one country but many countries, and that her artistic manifestations are the fruits of various races with their subsequently varying religions and social systems. The two forms which we have previously treated are both of South India. Here the basic religion is Hindu, and it teaches "action without action." Hinduism is calm and incorporeal and poses no material problems. The art-expressions it inspires are based on spiritual inspiration and effect.

Let us now examine the leading dance-art of North India. Here frequent invasions have left a hodgepodge of religious beliefs. Strongest among these is Mohammedanism, which spread over India from Iran between the eleventh century and the eighteenth century. Now the Prophet Mohammed is a man of action; his Paradise is gained through deeds rather than through meditation. In the North, then, we have action strongly influencing art-expression. At the same time, the protagonists of this art are a race of people long rich, living in a moderate climate, and themselves active as warriors, merchants and travelers. What more logical than that their art-expressions should pose great technical problems?

Northern Nāṭya is far less austere than the southern form from which it sprang. It is more human in subject matter and more worldly in technique. Most representative of the several schools of North India is the Kathak. Here, as in other, less-developed, types, little remains of the old Hindu Nāṭya save brief sequences of abhinaya which show the favored pantomimes of the South; such as Kṛishṇa, the gopīs, the peacock. Mohammedan influence is so apparent that, at times, Kathak appears pure Arabian in spirit. Surely the Turco-Afghan conquerors brought with them certain acrobatic dancing sometimes seen in North India—the Batasas, which is danced on lumps of sugar without breaking them; sounding of the kiṅkiṅī all at once or separately, and this without visible motion of the body; designing with the toes, while dancing, a peacock in meal scattered on the floor; or the complicated technique of moving the achkan and the gargari skirt.

[23] Hastas typical of Sadir Nautch can be found in Figures 3, 4, 10, 16, 21, 24, 26, 34, 40, 41, 61, 74, 77, 79, 82, 83, 90, 114, 115, 126, 132, 138, 142, 147, 155, 158, 159, 162, 164, 167.

Three different patrons of art (Vittala, Bhava Bhatta, and Gopala Nayak) tried during the sixteenth century to combine authoritatively the Bharata Nāṭya form, which was, of course, the original art, with the new hybrid dance, but without success. It is supposed that Kathak dancing is a derivative of kathakalakshepa, a South Indian dance form with much nṛtta and little abhinaya. Indeed, pantomime is relatively unimportant in Kathak, virtuosity being entirely in the feet. It is a dance of tālas and speed in doubling, counterpoint and syncopation are much admired. The dance has two parts, the torahs and the gaths. The torahs are rhythmic sequences of doubling and trebling time with the belled feet in a way which would correspond to our quarter, eighth, and sixteenth notes. The gaths are pantomimic gestures and depict simple scenes of everyday life; flying a kite, snake charming, drawing water. All the gaths are done in Lokadharma.

A complete knowledge of the tālas is indispensable to the Kathak dancer. It might be well to explain here as briefly as possible something of the tāla system of India. Indian music is scanned, not beaten. It is based on recurrent accent, not on pulsation. For the westerner the only hope of ever feeling this rhythmic pattern is to try to forget all his conscious and unconscious training of counting beats. Theoretically there exist several hundred varieties of tālas, but only about thirty-five of these are in common use. The titles differ somewhat between the North and the Peninsula. Each tāla is composed of an āvard, or rhythmic group of syllables. Half this āvard is called a vibhāg, and generally comes to about what one bar of our own music would be in the same pulsation. A mātrā is a unit of time. There are two mātrās to a long beat, and one to a short. Within the āvard are khālīs, or blank measures, tāls or accented measures, and the sama (or samas), which is the rhythmic climax. The sama is so-called because it is "complete"—which means that from time to time the singer, or rāga-player, and the tabla-player coincide on it. There are three different layas (tempi); viluhita (slow), maddhija (medium), and druta (fast). For purposes of clarification let us apply these basic theories to a common tāla. Tritāla (or tintāl) has four mātrās. It has three tāls and a khālī. The sama is on the first syllable of the āvard. It can be scanned as three shorts and a rest. This is the simplest of the various tālas, because it is not composed of shorts and longs in combination. Even if the dancer should triple the time, the steps come to even triplets. But in jhaptal, with its ten mātrās, tripling brings the dancer to beat three against two.

In executing a Kathak dance the dancer indicates to the musician his choice of a bola by means of rhythmic syllables. The syllables, apparently meaningless, convey to the tabla player whether to strike the daina (right-hand drum) the banya (left-hand drum), or both drums—and on which of their three tones to strike them. To perform a torah the dancer speaks to the drummer a bola. The drummer repeats this rhythmic phrase many times, while the dancer dances it, at first simply, then, with doubling tempi, trills, and counterpoint of the belled feet, until he is exhausted. He then may signal to the tabla player to cease and to leave the serangi, or esraj, playing the rāga alone, while he rests himself with the performance of gaths which are usually done with little or no movement of the feet. This is pure Kathak. Although the movements are somewhat feminine, the dancers are, more often than not, men. Originally this dance was performed by a sect of Brahmans who called themselves Kathaks. On religious occasions these Kathaks entertained the public with the recitation of epic poems—the Rāmāyaṇa and Mahābhārata, the Bhāgavata, and other Purāṇas. Their reading was liberally decorated with songs or musical passages, and all was enhanced with both abhinaya and descriptive hastas.[24]

Various Other Schools

In South India there exist, besides the important schools of Sadir Nautch and Kathakali, several other fine forms of dance and dance-drama.

Tirukuthu of Temil Nadu is a dance-drama so old that it is said that the following schools of Nāṭya have proceeded from it: Kathakali, of Malabar; Yakshagaṇa of Karnataka; and Telugu Vīthināṭaka of Andhra. Next to Kathakali, the best-known of these is the Yakshagana. This is a dance-drama presented by means of song, dance, and abhinaya. The themes are largely those of war, the actors thundering about the stage and performing very vigorous dances. The repertoire includes about fifty dramas, besides all the Rāmāyaṇa and the Mahābhārata, episode by episode. Unlike the Kathakali, it permits on the stage a clown, who interpolates sentiments of his own in reference to the happenings on the stage for the sake of provoking laughter in the spectators.

The dance school called Kuchipudi is much like Sadir Nautch save that it is more vigorous in character and that it has fewer complications in the floor contacts. But the general style is very similar to the lāsya dance already treated, both in the refinement of the movements and in the beauty and clarity of the hastas.

[24] Hastas typical of Kathak can be found in Figures 8, 13, 19, 76, 81, 85, 87, 89, 91, 144, 146, 160, 163, 194.

Brahman priests of Vishnu execute, in the month of Mṛgaśīrṣa, the Bhāgavata Melā Nāṭaka. By means of abhinaya these priests tell Vaiṣṇavaite legends set to music. The performances take place in the forests of Sulamangallam and Uttukado and in the town of Mangalam in the district of Tanjore.

In the north of India the Manipuri dance was the first[25] to meet with social approval when once the great renaissance had begun. Even today it is the form which best pleases the society ladies of India, since it is charmingly lyric in movement and not at all difficult of technique. Few of the hastas are used and these few only for decorative effect.

Inimitable are the dances of the Marwari women, those bangled and ankleted ladies who wear the wide gargari skirt long famous in all the world. Their popular dance is strongly Arabian in character, being full of spinning turns and subtle coquetries.

There are many characteristic dance-dramas in the north of India. In Mathura there is the picturesque institution of the Rasadharis, which is performed by Brahmans and which represents events in the life of Kṛishṇa. In Benares the popular play is the Rāmalīlā, which tells tales of the hero Rāma. In Maharashtra (western India), the play best-known is called Lalita; in Gujarat, Bhavai (similar to Tirukuthu, and including a clown); in Bengali, the Yatras; in Kurmachala, the Harischandra; in Nepal, the Gandharva Gaṇa (much like the Yakshagana, and said to be the creation of the literary king, Jagajjyotir-malla). The Lạlita and Bhavai plays are composed of short pieces which are considered very vulgar. These "local sketches" break the rules of "stage-decencies" laid down by Bharata. The Muni prohibited the performance of actions which did not contribute to the elevation of the spirit of the watcher, such as long journeys, murders, rebellions, eating, disrobing, sexual relations, and such things.

The New Dance of India

Quite recently—a score of years ago—there sprang up in India a new form of the ancient art of dancing. This is as it should be, for an art unrevivified becomes an empty shell, a mummy.

"It appears that even in Bharata's time the great art degenerated to the level of vulgar rustic performances of the type of Silpaka and Dombaka, losing all its original sanctity and dignity."[26] The classic dance fell on evil days in India, as

[25] See p. 20.
[26] B. V. and P. S. Naidu Tandava Laksanam (Madras, 1936), Introduction, p. 5.

it did in the West. We know what was our opinion of dancing and dancers at the end of the 1800's; the same opinion prevailed in India. The dance, performed by courtesans, flourished when the courtesans were the mistresses of kings and as such were surrounded by culture. But when kings disappeared, courtesans became prostitutes, yet still were the finest dancers. So, little by little, as the culture and mentality of the dancer lowered, the art she practiced lowered not technically, but spiritually. And so the dance fell into bad odor, until it was viciously attacked by reformers who tried to suppress the art altogether.

The well-known writer and aesthete Raghavan says, "Let the dancers of India resort to some traditional master of abhinaya to learn the whole foundation and science of the thing, steep themselves in the tradition of Indian art, culture, legend, and literature, and then devise new forms." While in the Nāṭya Śāstra the master, Bharata, writes that "the guru must devise new forms to move with the changing times."[27] This is exactly what has come to pass, and a new school has appeared in India which may be called the New Dance of India. This young expression of an ancient art is rapidly growing in both North and South India with equal success.

Toward the beginning of this century Rabindranath Tagore, then living in his Abode of Peace, a mansion some hundred miles from Calcutta, started a small school of the arts with five students enrolled, one of whom was his own son. In 1917 the poet, on a visit to Sylhet, saw an exhibition of Manipuri dancing and was so delighted with it that he brought back to his school two teachers of Manipuri. This was the birth of the renaissance of the Indian dance, although it was several years before the students of dancing would consent to appear in public. Finally Tagore wrote a special play, entitled *The Worship of the Dancing Girl*, which was produced in Calcutta, and from that time on more and more distinguished persons came forward to fight for the nobility of Indian dancing. Today the students of Santiniketan (Tagore's university) tour in every part of India, giving plays of song and dance written by the great poet himself.

In Malabar another great poet, Vallathol, fights to stem the decay of Kathakali and Mohini-attam. With a greater insight and a broader vision of the world, Uday Shan-kar is today laying the foundation of a new school of music and dancing. To this great artist goes the full credit for bringing to the West the beauty of his country's dance-art, as well as for his magnificent share in the general renaissance of the dance in India.

[27] This ruling is to be found in the ninth chapter, slokas 151–52 of the Nāṭya Śāstra.

The protagonist of India's New Dance uses the more comprehensible forms of aṅgikâbhinaya; the whole gamut of the hastas, the mukhaja, which is not too delicate to be observed in a modern theater; the gaths and torāhs of Kathak, and the lyricism of Manipuri. With this technical equipment he tells tales from the ancient classical subjects and adds *divertissements* based on everyday Indian life. He selects costumes and music carefully, always respecting basic tradition and style. He differs from the classical dancer in that he discards certain old rules which do not appeal to the pace and temper of modern life, even in India. If the orchestra follows the old ways and appears on the stage, its members are appropriately costumed and aesthetically disposed to aid the choreographic tableau. Old forms were very long and rather monotonous, and so nṛtya as well as nṛtta is presented in the modern school with a regard to length as well as crescendo. Many details written as rules in the Nāṭya Śāstra have been changed "to move with the changing times." There has been tasteful accenting of the classical technique, adaptation of the classical costumes, selection from the classical subjects, an application of the music, and above all shortening and lightening both of the evening's performance, and the numbers thereon. But all these changes must be made only by one who is well versed in all the classic rules and traditions, else is broken one of the first canons of art—to depart from classical forms through strength and not through weakness. Whoever disregards this rule courts his own downfall and retards the healthy growth of the art he seeks to practice. If a modernist statue is to have artistic value, it must be made by an artist who knows anatomy and departs from reality only to gain a specific effect, not by one who makes anatomical errors because of ignorance or lack of technique.

"In the fullest appreciation of this supreme art of Dance lies the touchstone of the highest aesthetic enjoyment and a properly evaluated scale to measure the nation's artistic achievement."[28] I dare say there is no other existing dance-art with such a wealth of tradition from which to draw. It needs only the pulsing blood of eager pride to bring it to a newer, greater glory.

TECHNIQUE

When one desires to learn a dance in the Occident, one is told, "I will teach you the steps"; in the Orient the teacher says, "I will teach you the hands." This is the fundamental difference, physically, between the art of the East and that

[28] G. K. Seshagiri, "Introduction" to the official publication of the *Congress Music Festival* (Madras, 1937).

of the West. By this I do not mean to imply that the technique of the lower limbs in the Hindu dance is left to the whim or natural grace of the performer, as is true of the technique of the arms in some forms of western dance. On the contrary, the technique of the lower body according to Bharata Nāṭya has been very scientifically broken up into component parts, and a complete muscular control of each is tabulated and learned. For example: bhūmya maṇḍala pāda (positions of the feet on the floor) are nine; these are comparable to the five basic foot positions of the ballet. The ākāśa pāda (positions of the feet in the air) are five; these control the position of the ankle, arch, and toes—a complete and expressive technique. The sthānaka sthāram (basic attitude of resting positions) are, according to the authority, from nine to fifteen; there are also the bhūmya cārī (movements of the feet on the ground) which are typical of Sadir Nautch; the ākāśa cārī (movements of the legs in the air) which are typical of Kathakali; the gati (gaits), which are as varied and numerous as the type of locomotion in man and beast; the bhrāmarī (spiral movements), the utplavana (leaps) and the pādapārśvakūṭṭanam (rhythmic beats of the floor contacts) typical of Kathak. There are of course endless combinations of all these.

But in spite of this complete and difficult system of control the lower limbs are used primarily as a rhythmic accompaniment to the amazing technique of the upper body. Leaving aside the movements of the torso which include the kaṭi rechaka (waist positions), the kakṣa rechaka (shoulder movements), the pārśva rechaka (side positions), and the udara rechaka (belly positions), let us glance briefly at Nāṭya's mukhaja. To begin with, there are twenty grīvā rechaka or addiyams (postures of the head and neck) each with its various viniyoga (expressive meanings). There are three kinds of driṣṭi (glances): rasa driṣṭi (glances which give rasa), of which there are nine; darśanas (looks which give mood), of which there are eight; and asta driṣṭi (glances which show passing emotions), of which there are thirty-five. These driṣṭi control the expression within the eye itself; the puṭa (eyelids) are tabulated under eight headings, and the bhū (brows) under seven. The āsya rechaka (mouth) has thirteen positions to express the emotions; the nāsa rechaka (nose), six; the cibuka rechaka (chin), six. The infinite combinations of these seven parts of facial expression are capable of producing the entire gamut of human and godlike emotion down to the last subtle shading.

Before speaking of the hands I should like to mention that the vartanas (arm postures) which carry these hands are scientifically tabulated in the space-pattern. Sometimes they are expressive within themselves, as with the gaja arm

(Fig. 2), but more often they are used only to carry the pantomimic hand to the appropriate position. The hastas and vartanas are in no wise dependent on each other—that is to say, any hasta may be combined with any vartanam; but obviously, the pantomimic meaning of any given hand pose will change according to the position of the arm.

The hasta mudrās (hand poses) are of two kinds: asaṁyuta (single-handed poses) and saṁyuta (double-handed poses). Of the asaṁyuta, there were originally twenty-eight. These have been added to from time to time, until now there are currently in use about thirty-five. Each of these is capable of various meanings. For example the patāka hand on the breast (Fig. 174) means "I"; slanted downward (Fig. 183) it means "here"; perpendicular and static (Fig. 57), "exposition"; perpendicular and vyāvṛtta (Fig. 130), "refusal." The hand itself has not changed, only its position in space, yet the meaning has been clearly and completely changed. This is the simplest example of an endless variety of applications of the asaṁyûta.

The saṁyuta were originally twenty-four.[29] But today the poses of combined hands have grown incomputable: "It is said that there are as many hands as meanings."[30] Some aesthetes claim that a single-handed pose is one which retains its meaning whether used alone or in combination with another hand (for example, sūcī-mukha can indicate a flower stalk either alone *or* with the flower of the padmakośa hand atop it, as in Fig. 30) and that the original saṁyuta were only the combination of two of the *same* hands (for example, two patākas make the saṁyuta of añjali, as in Fig. 170). But with the passage of time another type of combined hands has been added (for example, śikhara on siṁha-mukha means Siva, but separately they only mean "bull" and "man." See Fig. 187).

Today the more popular term for "hand pose" is "mudrā." This is because interest in iconography revived some time before interest in the dance, and the term "mudrā" is an iconographic one. Authors on Nāṭya use the term "hasta." Mudrās were first used by Sādhakas of the Tāntrik school to obtain the mud (peace) of meditation, for it is well known that rhythm excites rasa in the performer as well as in the watcher.

Roughly speaking, the hastas can be divided into three types. There are the purely descriptive gestures (Figs. 3, 21, 30, 35); the hastas which are drawn from

[29] Examples of these original samyuta can be found in Figs. 18, 20, 26, 27, 48, 51, 55, 60, 68, 73, etc.

[30] A. K. Coomaraswamy, *Mirror of Gesture* (New York, 1936), p. 57.

the sublimation of the natural gestures (Figs. 128, 174, 180, 182); and those based on the association of ideas (Figs. 55, 66, 81, 90).

Now, in using the science of the hasta-mudrā to build the work of art which is Nāṭya (dance-drama) or even Nṛtya, pantomimic dance, it is necessary that the combination of these hand postures has sauṣṭhava (beauty and grace). They must flow one into the other with an ease and beauty which will delight the eye of even that beholder who is ignorant of their actual meaning. Their expressiveness must be aided by the various and appropriate mukhaja and set upon the rhythmic, emotional support of the śarīra (technique of the torso) and cēṣṭa (lower limbs).

The beginning of the art of the hasta-mudrā was the mantra, or chant. At first, it was the priest who moved his hands in expressive gestures as he and his devotees chanted. Later, the devotees themselves began to move their hands also. Then the devadasi (temple-dancer) was created—a young woman who could move her hands with consumate beauty and skill.[31]

Even today the saṁgīta or mahāgītā (gesture-song), because of its very simplicity, is the finest example of the application of the art of abhinaya. In practice, the expressive movements of the hands, unadorned by any but the simplest of aṅgikabhinaya, are poignantly beautiful, as is the accompanying music. The principle which created it is as simple as that of the old nursery game: "Here are Mother's knives and forks; here is Mother's table; here is Mother's looking glass; and here's the baby's cradle." It is the expression of a thought by means of words and gestures combined. But are not all sciences built on truths as fundamental?

[31] Shrimati-Gauri of Mylapore, the finest temple-dancer in South India, is gray-haired and sixty. Partly because of her age and partly because it is not demanded of her art, she does only the simplest of thattadavu. But the beauty of her gesture-songs brings tears to the eyes. Her sweet, expressive face, and her subtle, wise hands are without equal. She is the embodiment of the art of the hasta-mudrā.

Introduction to Plates

IN PRESENTING this collection of Hindu hastas it has been my desire to select a certain number of representative poses and to show them in a manner both simple and direct. I have found in my conferences on the Indian dance that this complicated art is most easily clarified to the layman by showing a series of hastas in static poses. My desire, then, is to put this demonstration into readable form so that some of the infinite shadings of India's gesture-language may be compared and understood.

Selection has been difficult. I have tried to choose those hastas which are at once classic and clearly descriptive. The collection comprises poses from every part of India and some of iconographic origin, for the New Dance of India is drawn from all these sources.

In the photographs I have taken some care to give only the shadow of the facial expression which accompanies the hasta, partly because I did not want to distract attention from the hand-pose, and partly because each hasta may be accompanied by various and changing mukhaja. In some cases I have given several different hastas to express a single meaning. This is for comparative study of the various types of hastas and the style of various schools.

In giving with the plates the Sanskrit titles of the various hands I have been motivated by a desire for clarity, for through these titles it is easier to identify the exact positions of the fingers. Also, should the reader study Indian books on the same subject, he will find that these titles are often used as the exclusive means of pose description. The use of these titles, however, brings with it a certain difficulty. Written description of bodily movement is not always quite clear, and on the exact position of certain hands authorities sometimes disagree. I therefore warn my reader that, although I have followed what I consider the most widely used conception of a hand's title, he may find those who disagree with me on the *names* of certain hastas relative to their exact position.

All the titles herein given are in agreement with *The Mirror of Gesture* as translated by Dr. Ananda K. Coomaraswamy, save the following:

Apaviddha-sūci. The title can be found in Tandava Laksanam, a translation of Chapters VIII–XI of Bharata's Nāṭya Śāstra by B. V. and P. S. Naidu.

Kaṭhaka. This title is used in Manomohan Ghosh's translation of Nandikeśvara's Abhinaya Darpana.

Kathakali's ardha-candra. This title can be found in V. Raghavan's pamphlet on *Kathakali, and other forms outside Kerala.*

All three of these hand-poses are in current use in India. That they do not figure in all translations of Hindu Manuscripts on Nāṭya is probably due to the fact that Nāṭya is a living art, and hastas have been added to the original twenty-eight by āchāryas versed in aucitya.

As has been observed before, written description of bodily movement is not always quite clear, and it is true that some authorities disagree on the title of certain hand-postures. But it must be remembered that the translators themselves find disagreement in various manuscripts by the same author written on the same subject, but at different dates. This is not very surprising, since any conscientious artist must grow and refine both himself and the art he practices. Ghosh, translating from a palm-leaf manuscript of the thirteenth century, devotes several pages to his own difficulties in this line.[1] And, farther on in his book, he draws attention to points in which Nandikeśvara's manuscripts differ from the widely recognized Nāṭya Śāstra of Bharata.

> The language of hand-gesture has been enriched vastly in later times and the life-giving principle regarding these hastas is that they are directly derived from nature. . . . When one understands this secret and soul of hasta-abhinaya, and is a master of the emotions, endowed with a keen sense of aucitya, or appropriateness to place, time, idea, the form of art and the nature of the individual concerned, he becomes a master of hastas. He can invent suitable symbols for any new idea which may confront him. Bharata gave a few hastas and others that followed him some more, only to indicate; the world has to be studied and the artist must enrich himself with abhinaya for other objects and ideas. Bharata lays this down clearly and gives the means to create new symbols when an artist comes upon new objects and ideas.
>
> New symbols are created by observing the shape [Fig. 18], the characteristic action of a being [Fig. 11], the characteristic mark [Fig. 8] and by the nature of the class to which that being or object belongs [Fig. 56]. This will make the whole technique of what is called Indian classic dance as having its chief characteristic in hasta-abhinaya, easily

[1] Paragraph 3 of the Introduction to his edition of the Abhinaya Darpana.

intelligible and most intelligent. . . . He [Bharata] says: "What I have not said here must be taken from the world; therefore the world is the authority or proof for dramatic presentation; therefore the world must be made the source, the proof, the authority and the measure for valuation of success by those doing Nāṭya."[2]

The titles of the hand-poses, bestowed in the spirit of description, were given as a means of convenience to the naṭa, the guru, the āchārya, and the sūtradhāra. Since they were given as a convenience, it seems futile to make them a burden by launching long arguments as to their application. This book treats the hasta-mudrā kinetically and aims to clarify and to make workable the hand-titles. I have presented asaṁyutas and saṁyutas which are in use in India today. I myself have seen the hasta-mudrās in the following plates performed by authoritative dancers and teachers and used to convey the viniyogas which are herein given.

The hand-language of India is as complete and expressive as any spoken language. I myself, speaking no Tamil, have conversed with my teacher and colleagues by means of hasta-mudrās. I have found them adequate, not only in discovering the underlying principles of my instructor's methods, but even in carrying on the long, feminine, social conversations which were necessary to convince my fellow students that even a "meat eater" could be a rather nice sort of person. Vallathol, the great poet who has revived the Kathakali form in Malabar, is deaf and so converses entirely by means of the beautiful gesture-language of India.

In my many years of devotion to Bharata Nāṭya, I have not found any book similar to this *Gesture Language of the Hindu Dance* of mine, and so it is my hope that these pages will fill a need and because of their very simplicity be an aid to the better understanding of an art which has the power to give to both performer and watcher an integrated strength of spirit which is unique.

[2] V. Raghavan, "Nāṭyadharma and Lokadharma," in the *Journal of Oriental Research* (Madras), Vol. VII, Part 4.

Hasta Prāṇa

THE WORD "prāṇa" means "the breath of life." "Hasta prāṇa," then, is the breath-of-life of the hand-pose. It is the movement or position which gives "life" or meaning to those hastas to which it is applied. For example, in conveying the idea of spring by means of hastas, patāka hands (see p. 30) start in apaveṣṭita to indicate the earth; they then perform udveṣṭita and open in saṁdaṁsa (see p. 37) to indicate the blossoming of the earth.

The hasta prāṇa are as follows:

(1) Kuñcita (bent): curling fingers inward.
(2) Prerita (direct): turning fingers backward.
(3) Recita (revolved): rotating the hand on the forearm.
(4) Apaveṣṭita (twisted down): turning the palm downward.
(5) Udveṣṭita (twisted up): turning the palm upward.
(6) Puṅkhita (feathered): vibrating or trembling.
(7) Vyāvṛtta (turned back): a wagging or patting movement from the wrist.
(8) Prasaraṇa (outspread): relaxing or separating the fingers.
(9) Bhujaṅga (snake): fingers moving from kuñcita to prerita, giving a wavy movement to the back of the hand.

Every hasta can be executed in any of the above hasta prâṇa. At times the kuñcita pose changes very much the aspect of a hand. Nandikeśvara even gives a different name to mṛga-śīrṣa (see p. 32) in ardha-kuñcita (vyāghra: see Fig. 7). For comparative study of kaṭakā-mukha as it appears in prerita and kuñcita see figures below.

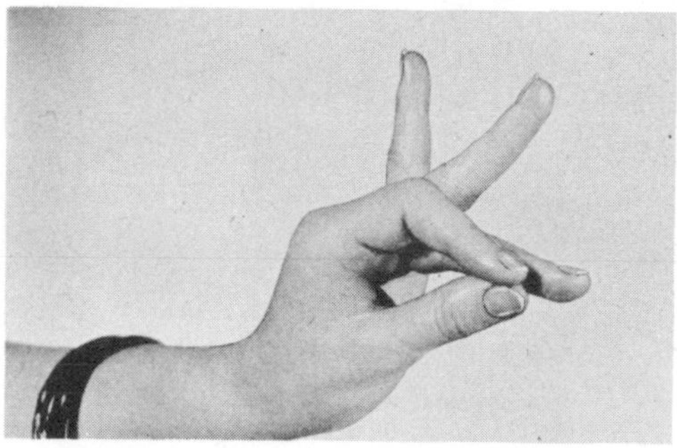

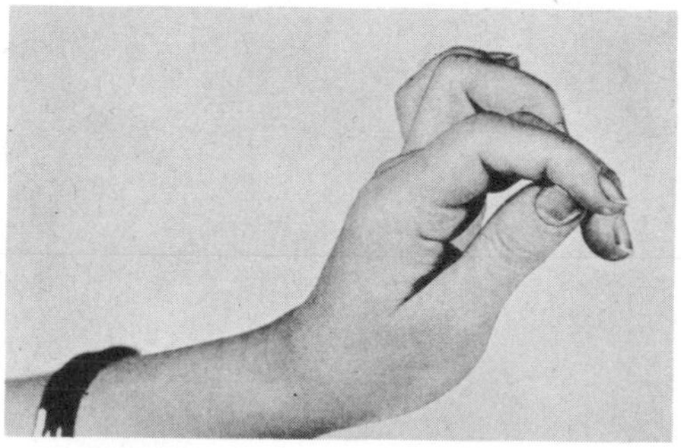

Asaṁyuta

AND SOME OF THEIR MANY VINIYOGA

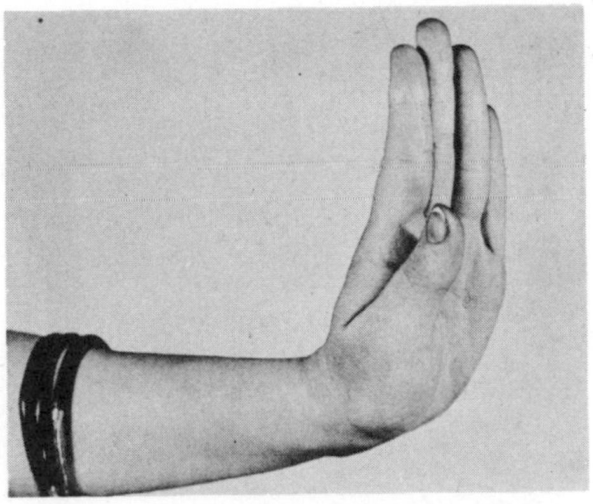

Patāka (flag)

I (Fig. 174); you (Fig. 175); exposition (Fig. 57); refuse (Fig. 130); earth (Fig. 183); past (recita from palm front to palm back); future (reverse action of "past"); "here," "this place" (Fig. 183); cloud (udveṣṭita above head); bosom (palm on bosom); cut (Fig. 115); underneath (palm down, move under); cheek (palm in, touch cheek); water (palm down, bhujaṅga); ear (palm front at ear); year (palm down, palm up, palm down); month (palm down, palm up); run (vyāvṛtta).

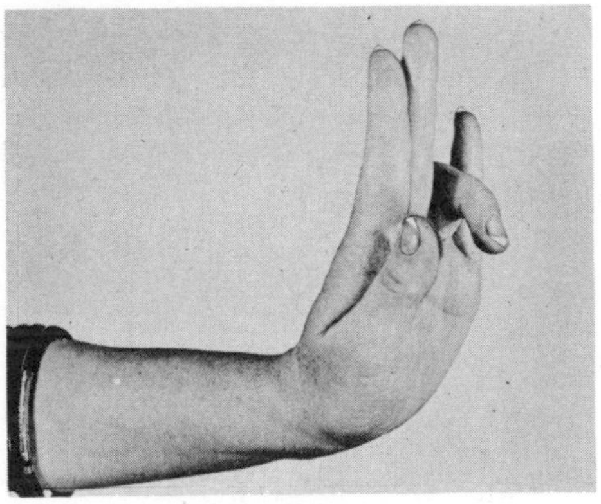

Tripatāka (three parts of a flag)

Flower on tree (Fig. 151); cow (prerita, palm down); "Come here!" (palm up, ring finger moving); rising flames (palm up, ring finger puṅkhita); union (opening and closing index and middle fingers); return (recita from palm front to palm back); descend (Fig. 183); doubt (touching heart with ring finger and moving hand in vyāvṛtta).

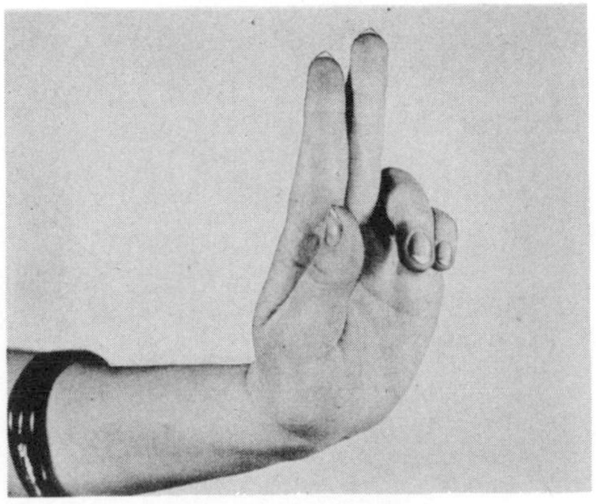

Ardha-Patāka (half-flag)

Dagger (Fig. 25); lightning (Fig. 40); yoga (Fig. 72); we two (Fig. 84, index and middle fingers moving); both or together (Fig. 84): river bank, falling leaves (palm down, index and middle fingers puṅkhita); cutting with saw (Fig. 115).

Ardha-Candra (half-moon)

Viṣṇu devotee (Fig. 190); mirror (Fig. 101); wiping sweat; plate (kuñcita, palm up); writing parchment; "Seize throat!" elephant ear.

N.B. Kathakali calls this hand "patāka"; traditionally it is often used for patāka.

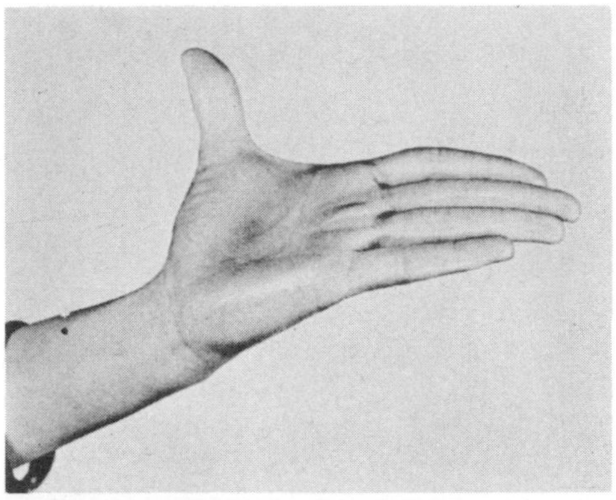

Candra-Kalā (digit of the moon)

Rest or meditation (Fig. 63); "Listen to me!" (angrily; vyāvṛtta, Fig. 182); moon (Fig. 186); Ganges (for patāka in Fig. 33); face (Fig. 100); measure (distance between thumb and forefinger).

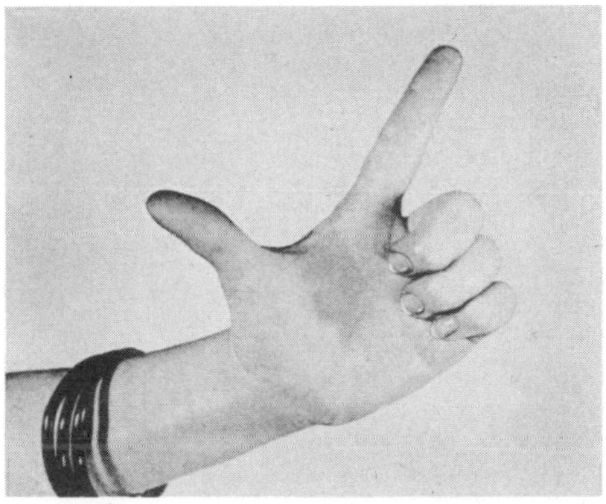

Sūcī-Mukha (needle)

Wife (Fig. 167); there (point toward); "What shall I do?" (Fig. 177); Rāvaṇa (Fig. 197); "Listen to me!" (gently, in vyāvṛtta); world (describe horizontal circle from left to right); nose (touch nose); I (boasting); pointing to a distance (above horizon-line).

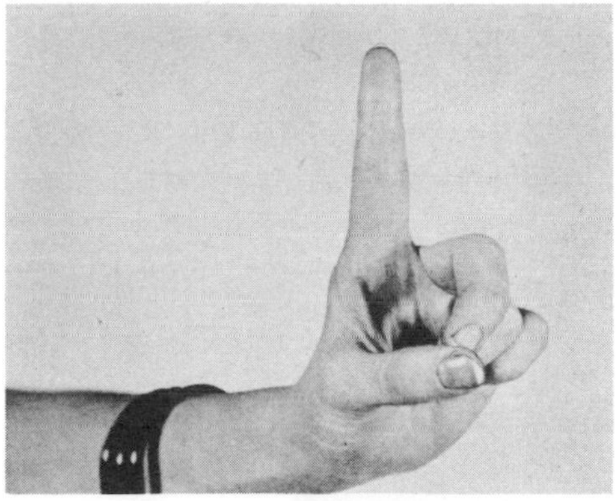

Mukula (bud)

Jackal (Fig. 5); lotus-bud (Fig. 31); to give or to feed (Fig. 156); humble speech (to mouth and outward), God of Love (representing his five arrows).

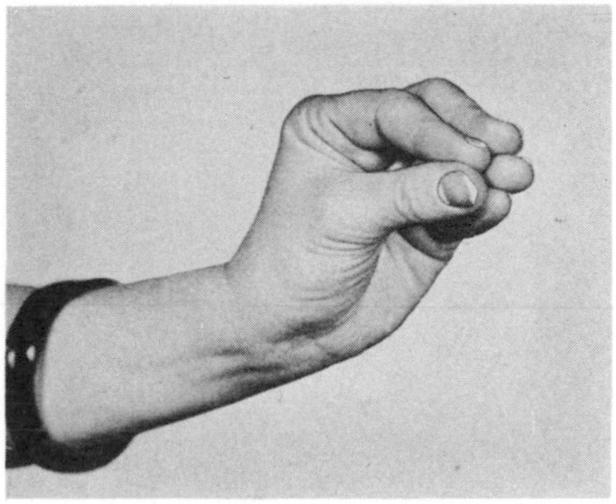

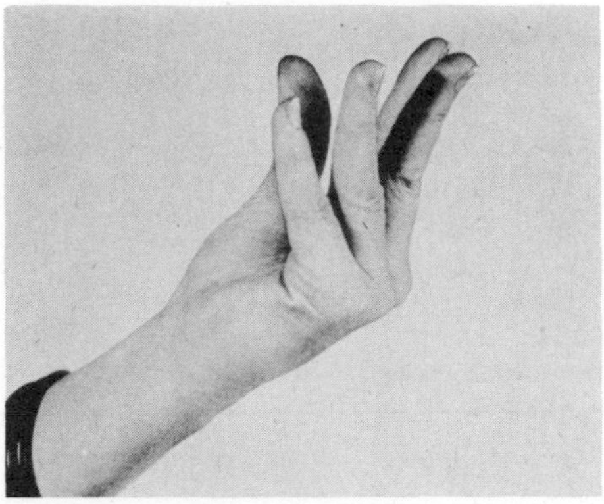

Padmakośa (lotus-sheath)

Lotus (Fig. 30); banyan-tree (turned downward); ball (hand held horizontally); bell (palm down and vyāvṛtta); rain of flowers (palm down and separate fingers puṅkhita); eat (padmakośa grasps food and mukula carries it to the mouth); scattering flowers (mukula grasps flowers and padmakośa scatters them).

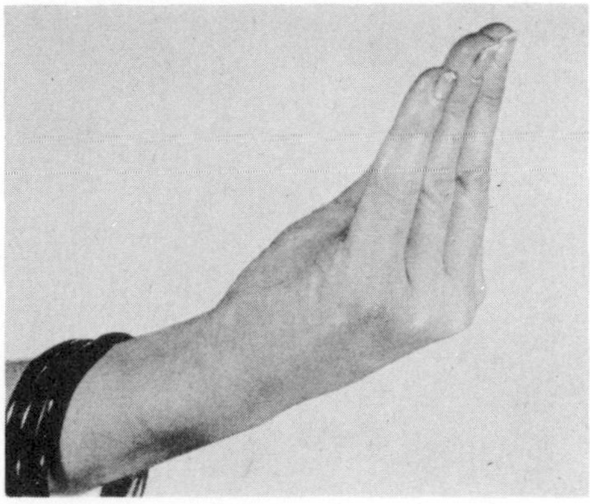

Sarpa-Śīrṣa (snake head)

Drink (Fig. 144); cobra (Fig. 16); hold a box (palm up); girl, or daughter, or child (Fig. 162); beyond (Fig. 168); bashful (conceal face); conceal (conceal object); washing face (scooping up water with sarpa-śīrṣa and passing sarpa-śīrṣa over face); sprinkling powder (palm up, puṅkhita); slowly (Fig. 57).

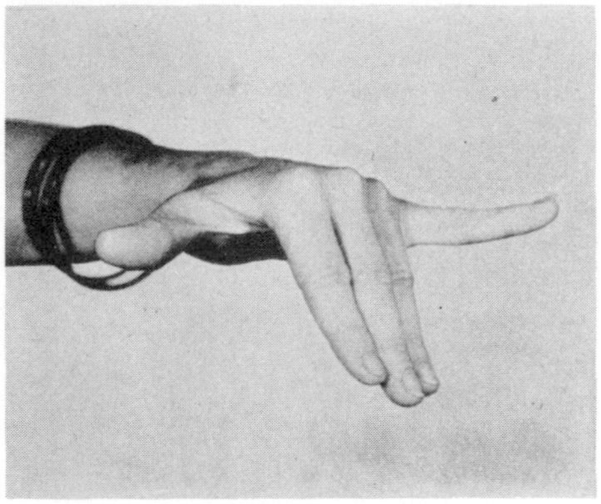

Mṛga-Śīrṣa (deer head)

Body (perpendicular); deer (horizontal, as in Fig. 1); three brow lines (pass across forehead); fear (before eyes and puṅkhita); putting henna on the feet (pass across feet); calling beloved (palm up and puṅkhita first three fingers); holding a stringed instrument (Fig. 161).

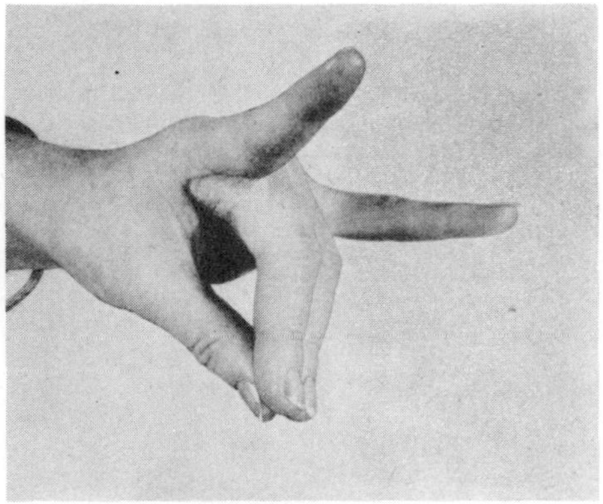

Siṁha-Mukha (lion face)

Cow (Fig. 1); tiger or lion (kuñcita); smell (palm up, under nose); eyebrows (Fig. 95); drop of water (palm down, puṅkhita); salvation (describe small circle over breast); hare (Fig. 6).

Muṣṭi (fist)

Grasp (Fig. 104); old person (Fig. 164); holding a shield (Fig. 165); riding (hold reins as in Fig. 103); steadfast (as Fig. 74); fighting; carrying away by force (as Fig. 194a); grasping hair.

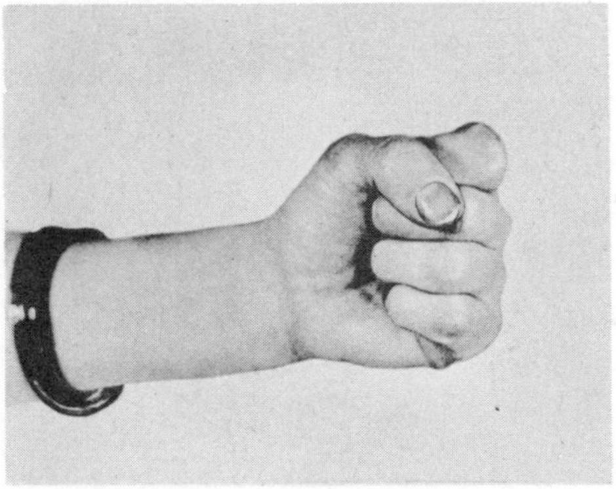

Śikhara (spire)

Establish (Fig. 74); man; killing ("thumbs down"); crow (Fig. 155); drink (Fig. 142); ancestor worship; "What is happening?" (Fig. 179); ringing bell (thumb up, ring); plying palmyra fan (thumb up, describe small circle); demure, amorous (thumb at chin); hair-knot (behind ear).

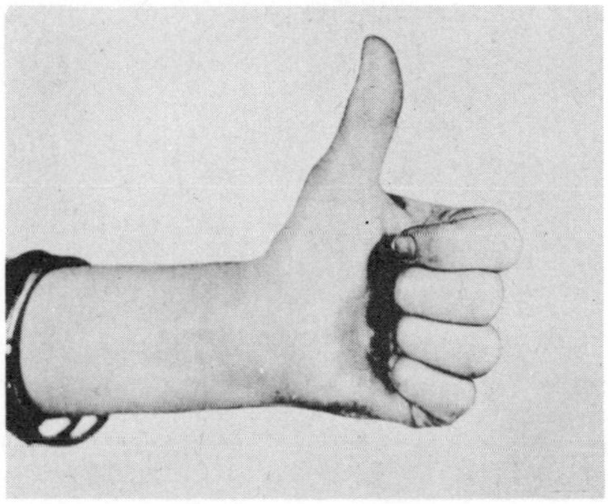

Alapadma (lotus)

Lotus (Fig. 32); love (Fig. 79); admiration (Fig. 91); mountain (Fig. 41); face (Fig. 100); crowned (Fig. 186); blessings of the gods (Fig. 191); listening to vibrant sounds (puṅkhita beside ear); palace (on patāka for earth); marriage (as "palace" except with patāka palm upward); full moon (Fig. 44).

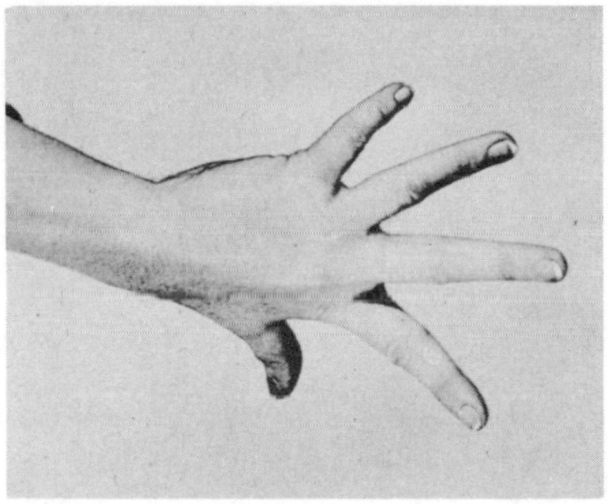

Arāla (crooked)

Fear (puṅkhita under heart); light offering (palm up, index finger puṅkhita); secret aversion (palm toward cheek, recita to palm outward); benediction (Fig. 57).

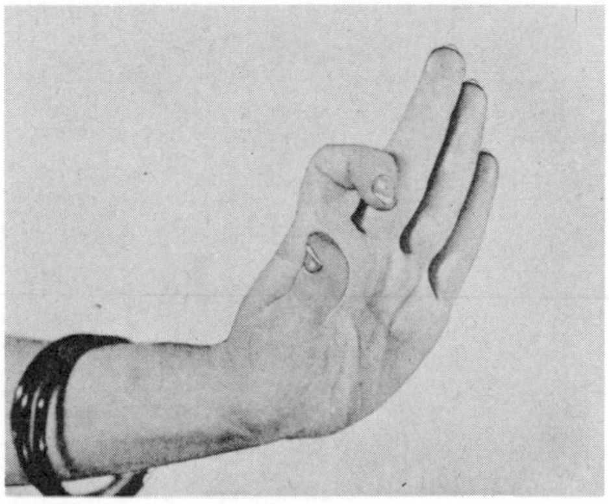

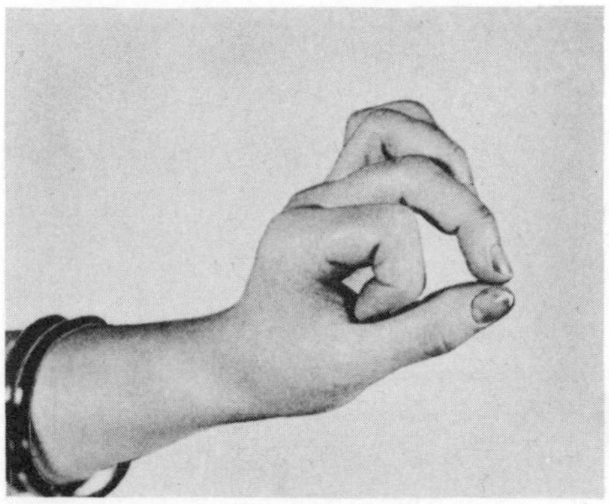

Bhramara (bee)

Bee (puṅkhita); secret (palm upward); unloosing garments; holding coral (Fig. 106); certain flowers (those of the papilionacea family); wing.

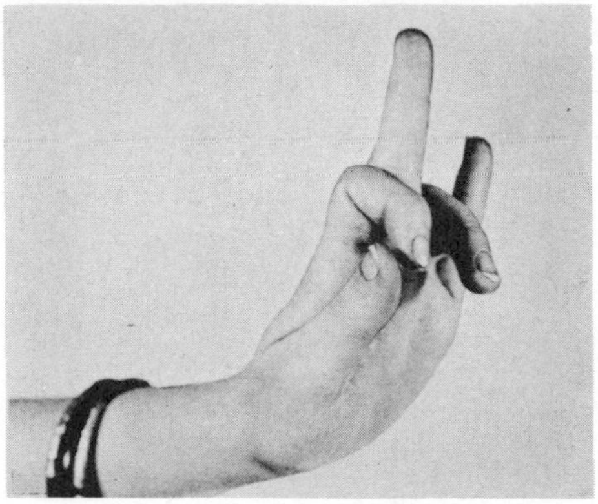

Śuka-Tuṇḍa (parrot's beak)

Turn over (from palm downward to palm upward); throwing a spear; butterfly (kuñcita and puṅkhita); flight of a parrot (puṅkhita); shooting an arrow (with śikhara for "bow"); violent mood (palm downward, puṅkhita under heart); remembering habitation (palm down, middle finger at temple. The other hand represents type of habitation: i.e. alapadma for "palace").

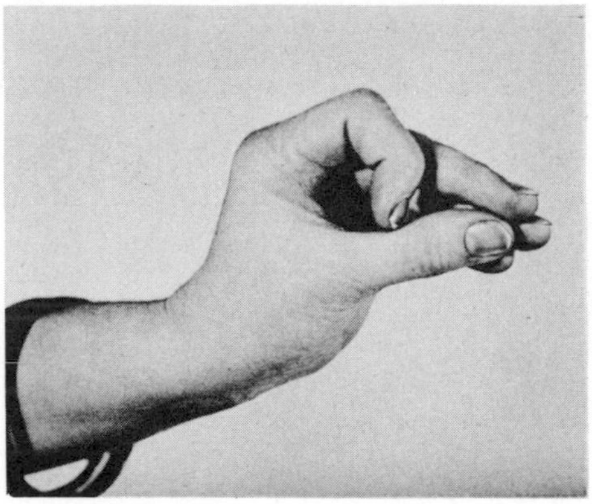

Tāmra-Cūḍa (cock's crest)

Domestic fowl; camel (vyāvṛtta); snail; drawing or writing poetry (with ardha-patāka for drawing board); the number three.

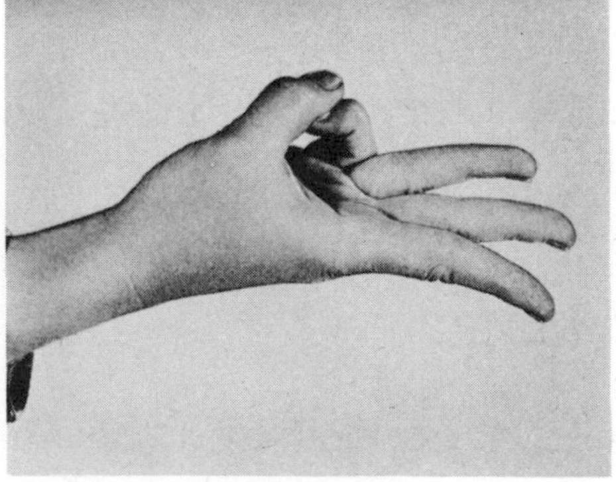

Triśūla (trident)

Śiva the three-eyed god (Fig. 184); three together (as Fig. 84); trident of Viṣṇu; rainbow (Fig. 38); the trinity of Brahmā, Viṣṇu and Śiva.

Kartarī-Mukha (scissor-face)

Separation of man and wife (Fig. 87); water buffalo (palm downward, prerita); scissors (clipping movement with first two fingers); stealing; death; sleeping alone (Fig. 54).

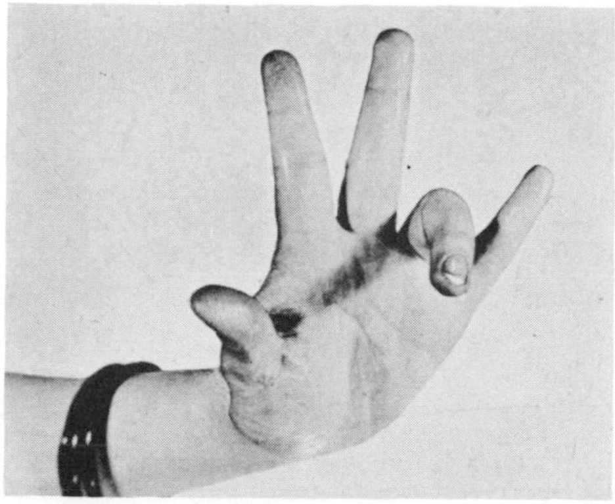

Kaṭakā-Mukha (crab-face)

Peacock's beak (Fig. 10); bird; stroking mustache (used for pride, boasting, masculine anger, or husband) (Fig. 114); draping sari (Fig. 128); holding pearls (Fig. 106); holding flowers (Fig. 151); to lead (Fig. 180); plucking (a flower, Fig. 151, a bowstring, Fig. 199).

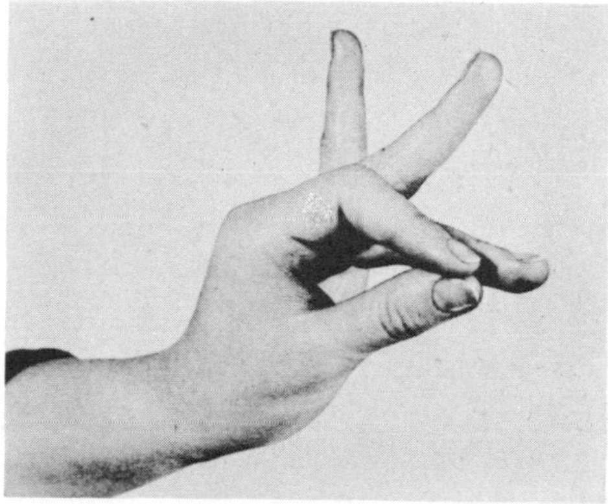

Kapittha (wood-apple)

Pulling (as Fig. 121); holding lotus of dalliance; Lakṣmī or Sarasvatī; grasping end of robe; offering incense or light.

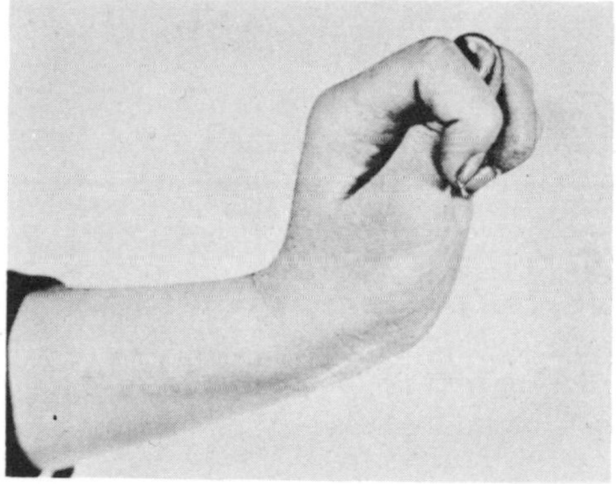

Catura (four-fingered)

Beckon (palm upward, vyāvṛtta); amorous torment (describe small circle over breast); scattering pūjā flowers (palm upward, palm downward); eye (touch corner of eye); think (touch temple with middle finger); sufficiency (Fig. 57); tip of ear (touch with middle finger); sorrow (cover eyes, palm inward); slow gait.

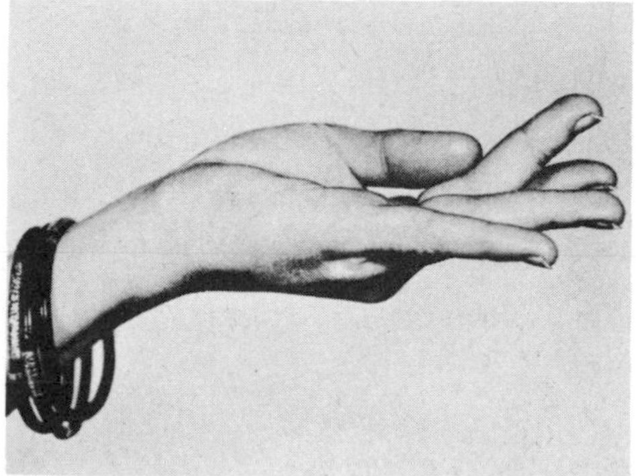

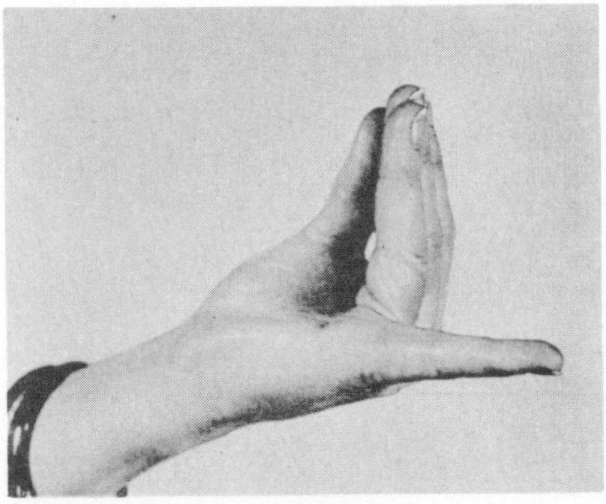

Haṁsapakṣa (swan-feather)

Step (Fig. 139); asking (Fig. 112, palm upward); "Come here!" (Fig. 124); bridge (palm downward); gathering (palm upward); the number six.

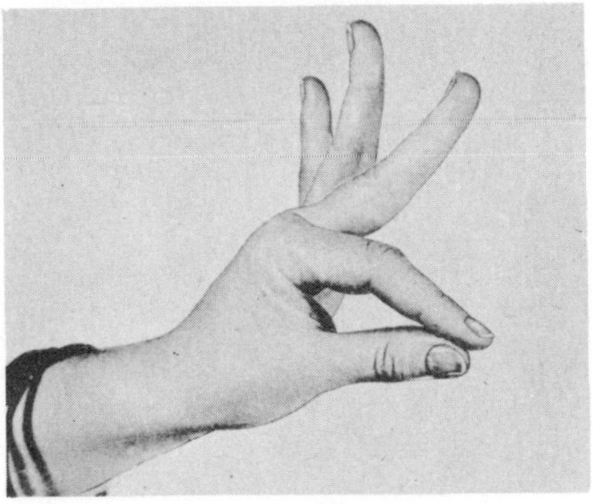

Haṁsāsya (swan face)

Love (Fig. 78); plucking (sitar or vīnā, Fig. 161; an arrow, Fig. 119); holding (garlands, Fig. 109; a bird Fig. 135; seduction, Fig. 52; a pen, Fig. 102); dancing (Fig. 160); "No!" (palm outward and fingers flying apart); sing (kuñcita near mouth); listening to music (kuñcita near ear).

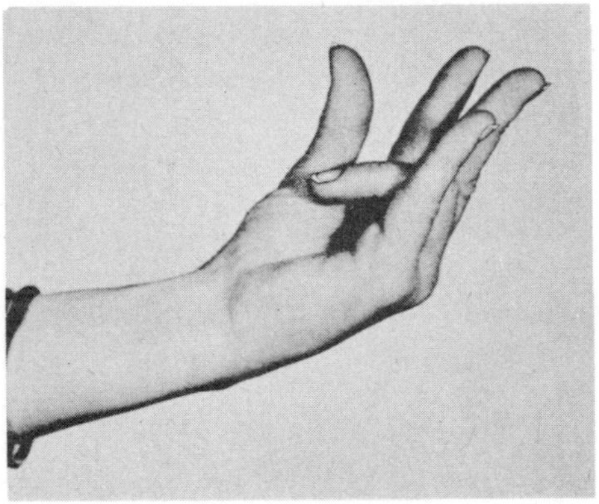

Lāṅgūla (tail)

Bee in lotus (palm upward); think (rest chin in fingers); small (palm outward); Kiṅkini (puṅkhita); water-lily (Fig. 44); partridge. This is sometimes written "Kāṅgūla."

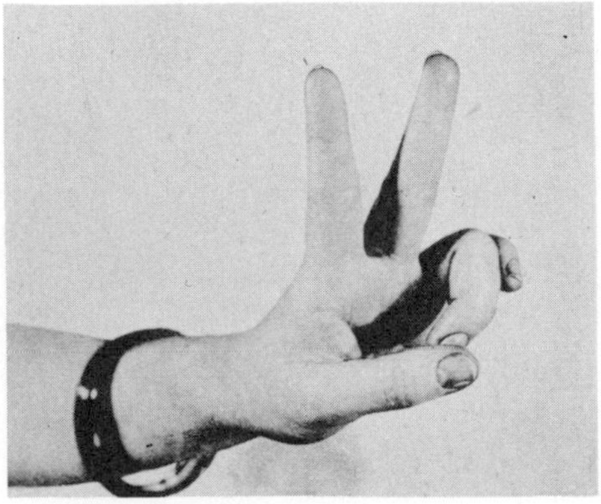

Mayūra (peacock)

An angry eye (Fig. 172); firefly (puṅkhita); wound (separating first two fingers); vine (recita, Fig. 35); peacock's neck, caste-mark (touch forehead with middle finger).

Saṁdaṁśa (tongs)

The saṁdaṁśa hand is padmakośa opening and closing. Belly (palm inward, in that region); fear (closed, palm to chest; open, palm outward); listening (closed, palm toward ear; open, palm outward); grow or sprout (palm upward); flies (the insects: puṅkhita); measuring worm (palm downward); spring (patāka; apaveṣṭita; for earth, followed by saṁdaṁśa, palm upward, for sprouts).

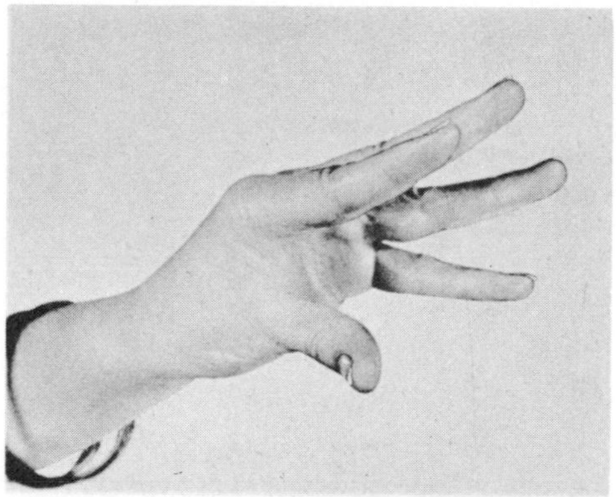

Kathakali's Ardha-Candra

Anger in heart (Fig. 49); showing (Fig. 127); washing (Fig. 150); sparkling water (palm down, puṅkhita).

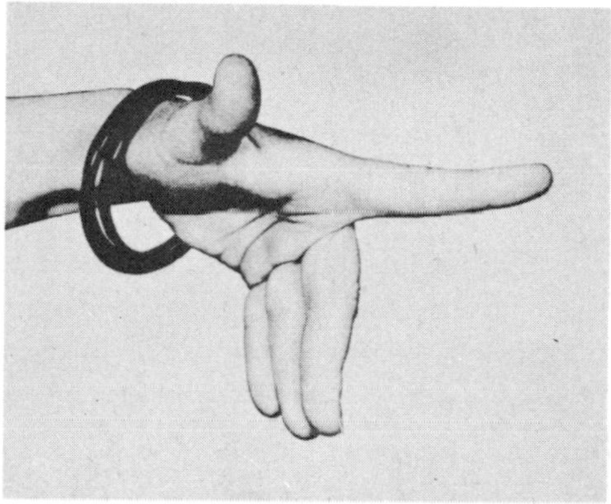

Urṇa-Nābha (spider)

Spider (as Fig. 164); peacock's-tail (Fig. 10); cloud (Fig. 36); grasping or catching (open and close); stealing; rain or mist (palm downward, separate fingers puṅkhita).

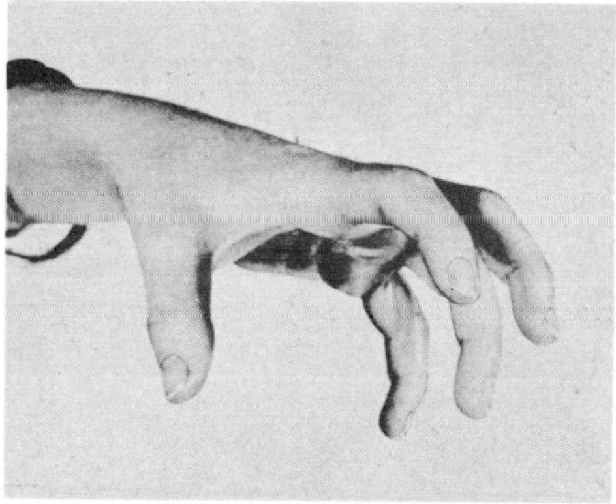

Apaviddha-Sūcī (inverted needle)

Look (Fig. 88); unscrewing (Fig. 94); holding (fire, kuñcita; lotus; jewels, puṅkhita); breaking (jar, Fig. 126; a flower stem, vyāvṛtta); a little (palm outward); face (circle face); earring (Fig. 99); bangles and bracelets (Fig. 97); dancing (at cheek, Fig. 158).

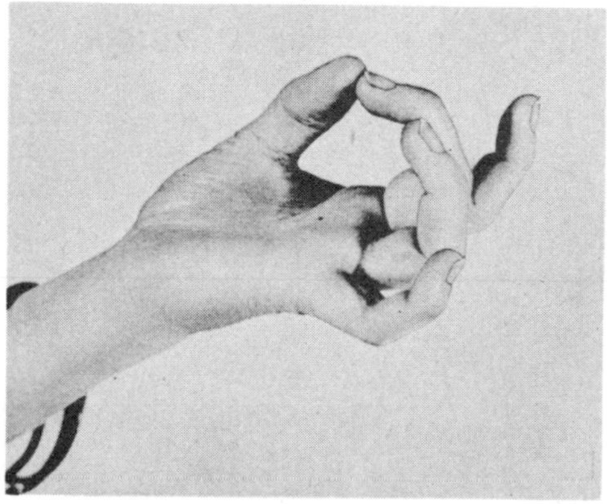

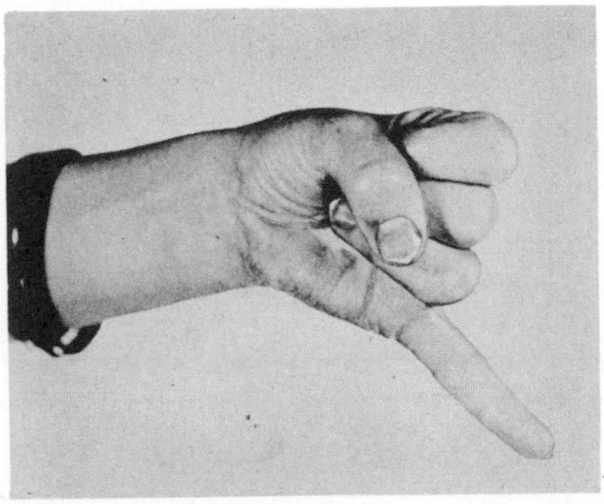

Bāṇa (arrow)

Elephant (Fig. 3); disgust (palm up at mouth, open to ardha-candra).

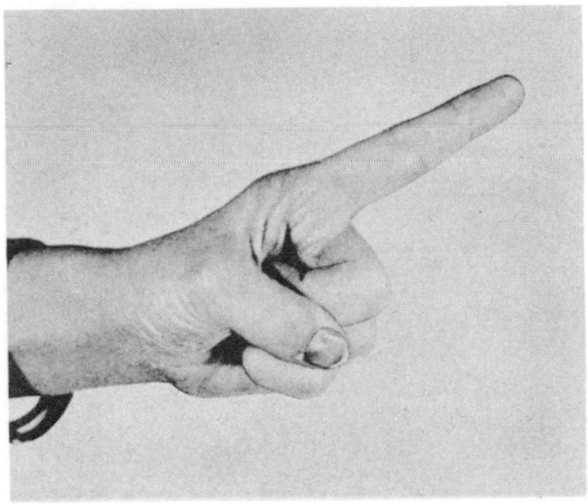

Ardha-Sūcika (half-needle)

This hand has the same usage as sūcī-mukha, save that it is more forceful. Kathakali calls this hand "Śikhara," and uses the Śikhara here given for "muṣṭi."

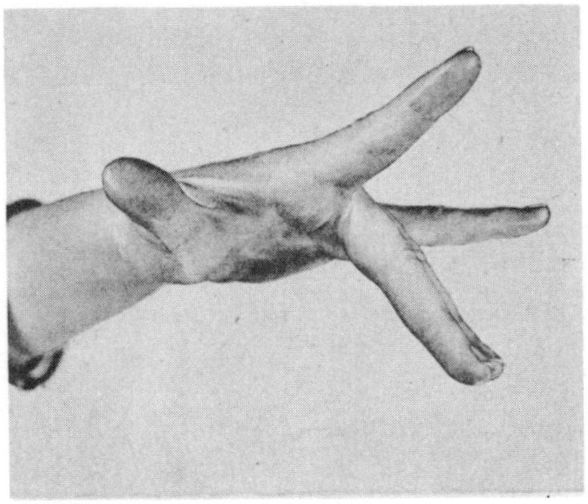

Kaṭakā (crab)

Wiping away tears (pass over eyes or cheeks); call from a distance (palm outward at mouth); elephant (vyāvṛtta).

Two Hundred Saṁyuta

AND THEIR VARIOUS VINIYOGA

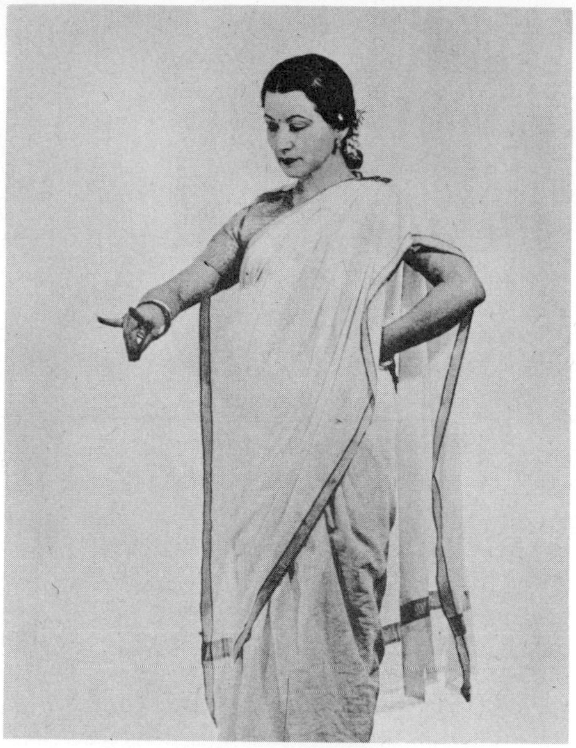

Fig. 1. Cow

Fig. 2. Elephant

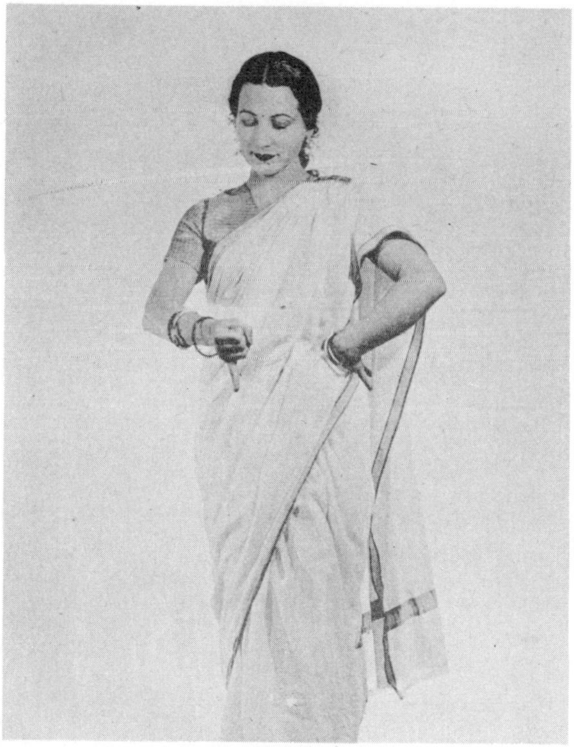

Fig. 3. Elephant

Fig. 4. Elephant

In Fig. 1 the hand is siṁha-mukha and the pose is static, or with a light movement (vyāvṛtta), to indicate the sway of the cow's head in walking. In Fig. 2 the right hand is tripatāka; the left arm in gaja. In Fig. 3 the hand is bāṇa. In Fig. 4 the hands are both kathakā. As saṁyuta they are called khaṭvā. The thumbs move slightly to simulate the beast's ears, while the hands may move from the wrists to represent the swaying of the head.

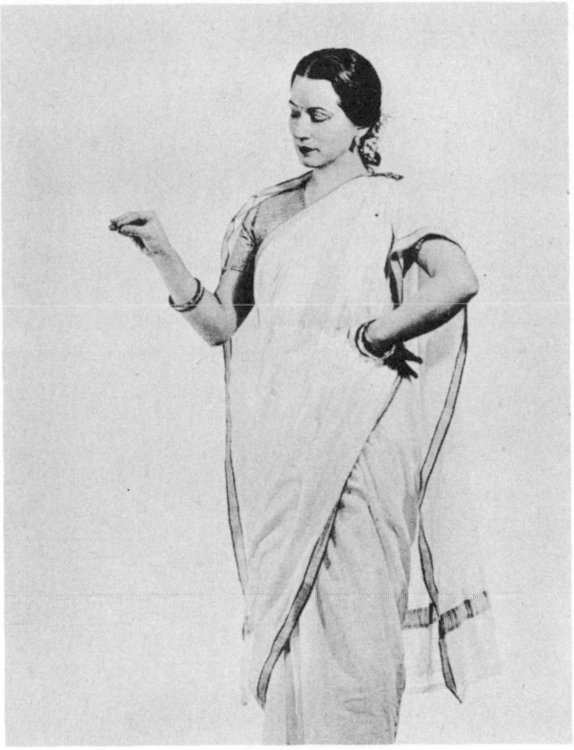

Fig. 5. Jackal

Fig. 6. Hare

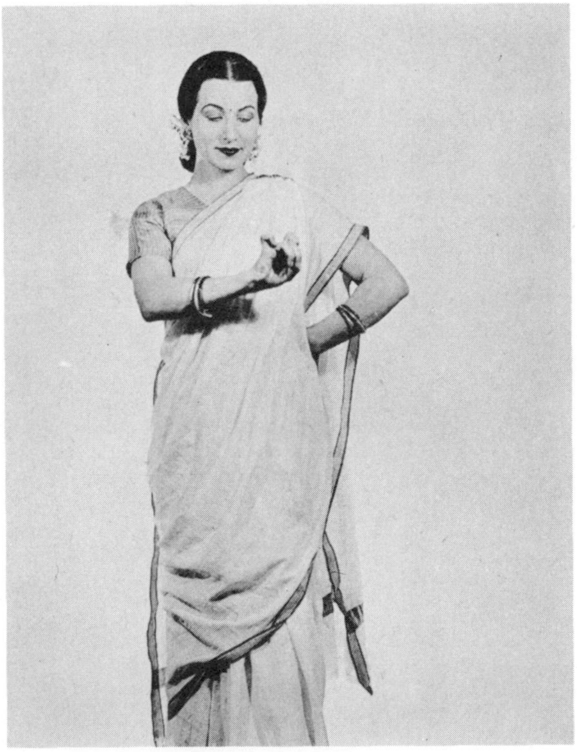

Fig. 7. Tiger

Fig. 8. Peacock

In Fig. 5 the hasta is mukula, and can be moved in vyāvṛtta. In Fig. 6 the hasta is siṁha-mukha, ardha-kuñcita. In Fig. 7 the hand is in siṁha-mukha, kuñcita. The hands in Fig. 8 are in prasaraṇa of patāka. Starting from directly above the head, they move simultaneously downward until they reach hip-height (the picture is taken about a third of the way through this movement). At the same time both hands move in vyāvṛtta. This indicates the outline of the spread tail of the peacock.

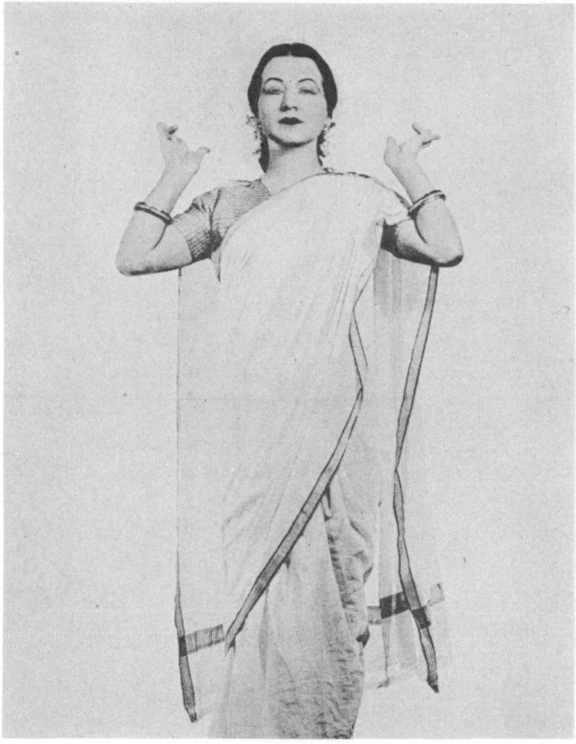

Fig. 9. Peacock

Fig. 10. Peacock

Fig. 11. Peacock

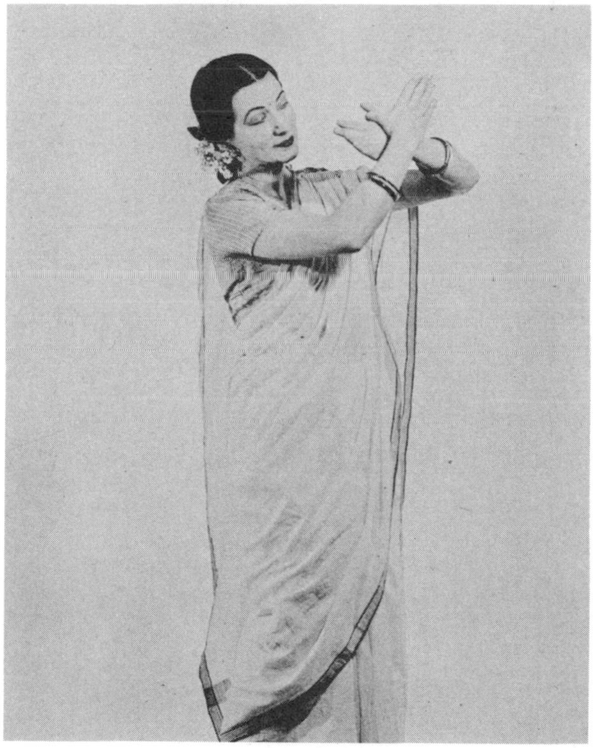

Fig. 12. Bird

Fig. 9 shows the hands in tripatāka (arāla is sometimes used). They are moved perpendicularly in vyāvṛtta. The right hand in Fig. 10 is in ūrṇa-nābha kuñcita; the left in kaṭhakā-mukha. In Fig. 11 the hand is in tripatāka. The head moves (prakaṁpita) from the shoulder toward the hand, which comes up to meet the chin. This represents the peacock preening his feathers. Fig. 12 shows ardha-candras in swastika, (saṁyuta: garuḍa). The hands move in vyāvṛtta to indicate flapping wings.

Fig. 13. Bird

Fig. 14. Cuckoo

Fig. 15. Bee

Fig. 16. Cobra

In Fig. 13 apaviddha-sūcī, interlaced, gives the effect of a fluttering bird. See Fig. 135 for another hasta representing "bird." In Fig. 14 bhramara and patāka, in svastika, indicate the bird's head and tail. In Fig. 15 bhramara hasta in puṅkhita imitates the bee. The hand in Fig. 16 is in sarpaśīrṣa (kuñcita) and represents the cobra's spread hood.

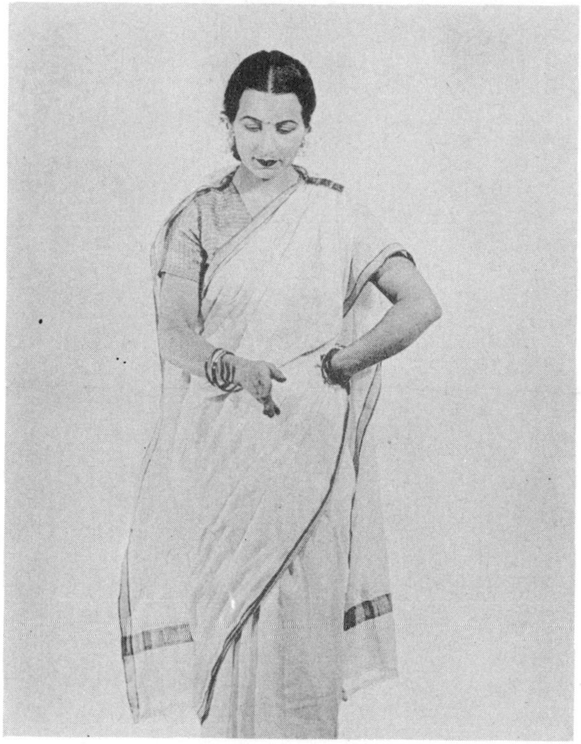

Fig. 17. Snake

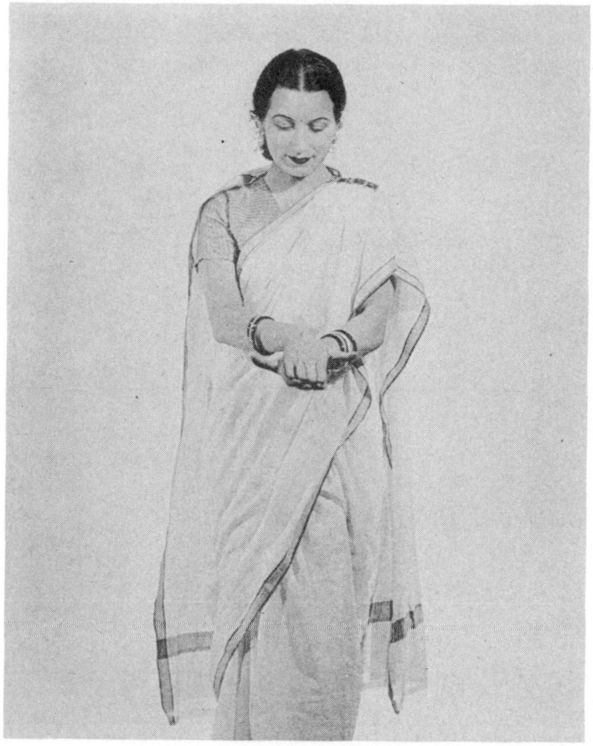

Fig. 18. Fish

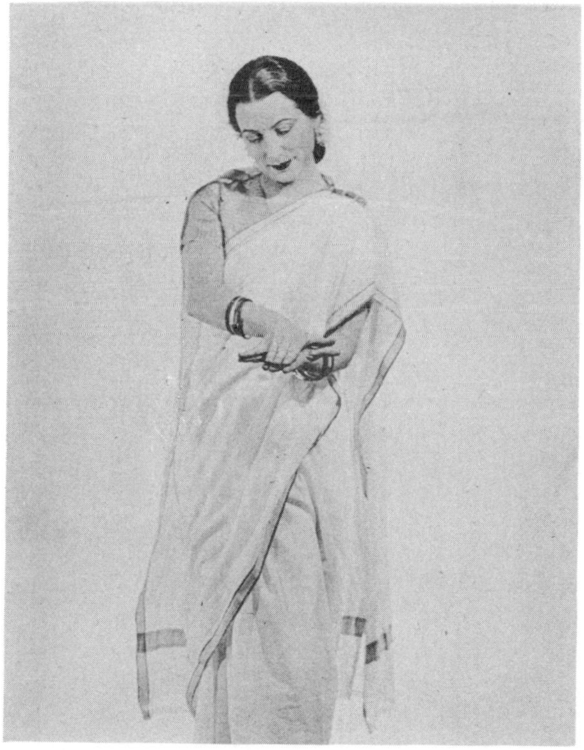

Fig. 19. Fish

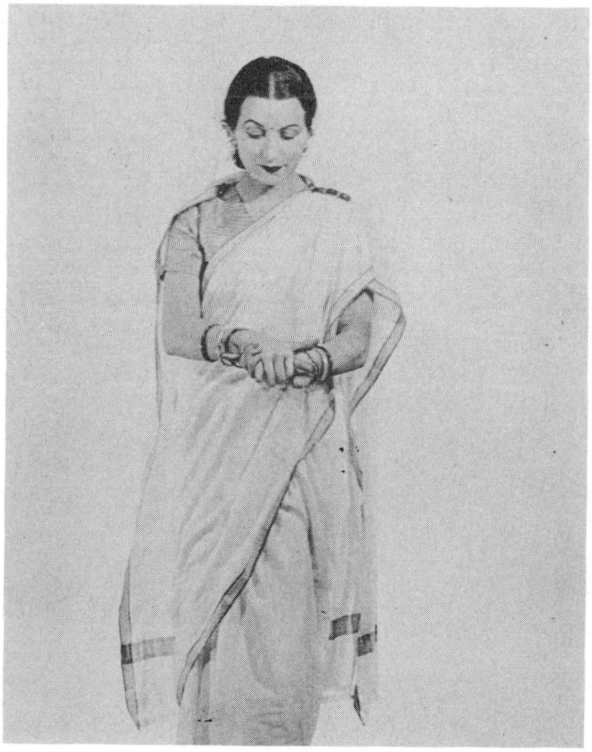

Fig. 20. Tortoise

In Fig. 17 the hand is in patāka. It moves from the wrist in subtle curves (bhujaṅga) to depict the crawling of a snake. In Fig. 18 the hands are in ardha-candra (saṁyuta: matsya). The thumbs move to simulate the fins. In Fig. 19 the hands are mṛga-śīrṣa. In Fig. 20 the hands are mṛga-śīrṣa interlocked (saṁyuta: kūrma). The thumbs and the little fingers move to represent the creature's legs.

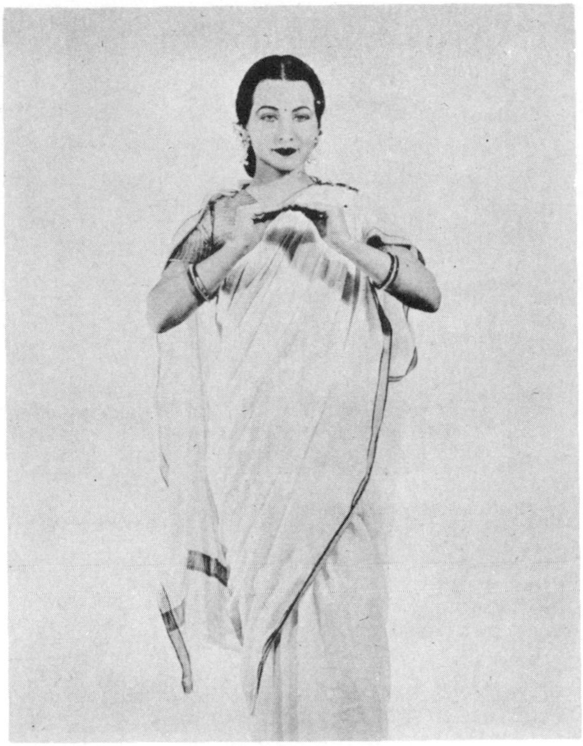

Fig. 21. House

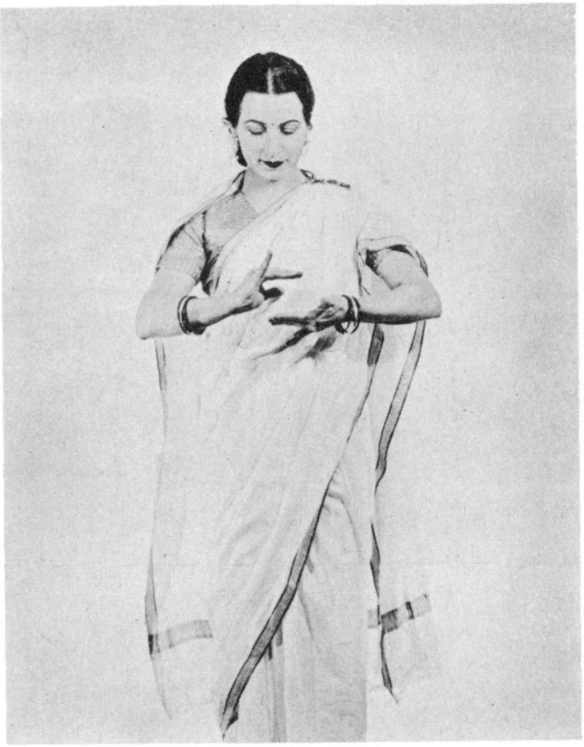

Fig. 22. Home

Fig. 23. Bed

Fig. 24. Bridge

In Fig. 21 both hands in sarpa-śīrṣa represent the line of India's flat-roofed houses. In Fig. 22 mṛga-śīrṣas, palms facing, indicate roof and bed. Fig. 23 shows both hands in siṁha-mukha. In Fig. 24 the right hand is in patāka, the left in mayūra. The left hand moves from contact with the palm of the right hand to the position pictured to indicate "bridging."

Fig. 25. Dagger

Fig. 26. Flute

Fig. 27. Flute

Fig. 28. Conveyance

The hand in Fig. 25 is in ardha-patāka. The hands in Fig. 26 are mṛga-śīrṣa in kuñcita (saṁyuta: kīlaka.) The flute depicted is the type used by snake charmers. The hands in Fig. 27 are again in mṛga-śīrṣa, this time depicting a flute of a different type. This hasta also indicates Kṛṣṇa, the Divine Lover, who plays the flute. (Saṁyuta: kṛṣṇa-avatāra.) Fig. 28 shows mṛga-śīrṣas, palms upward.

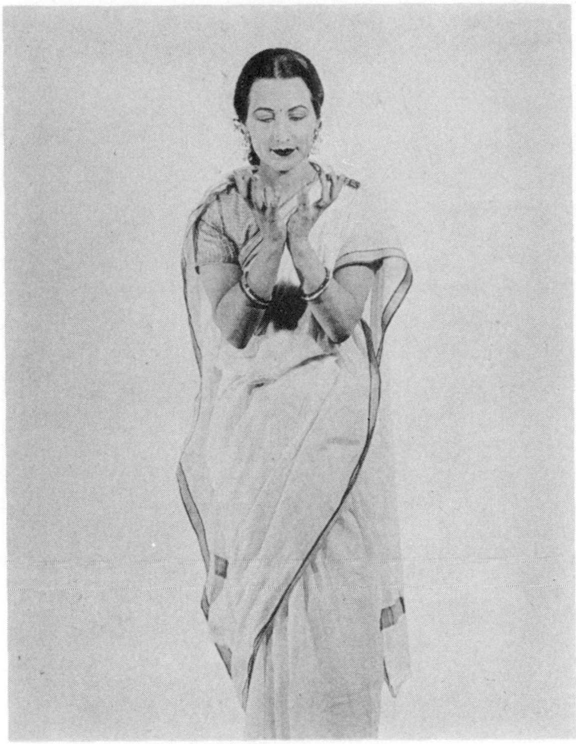

Fig. 29. Lotus

Fig. 30. Lotus on Stalk

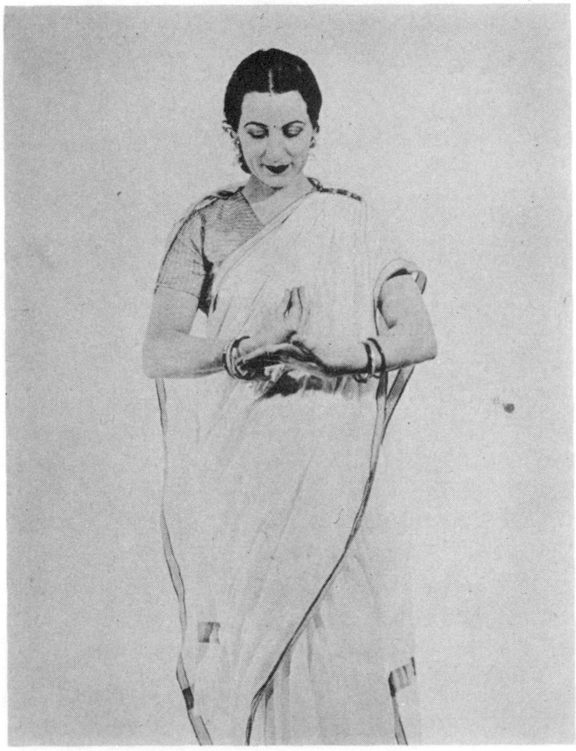

Fig. 31. Lotus Bud on Water

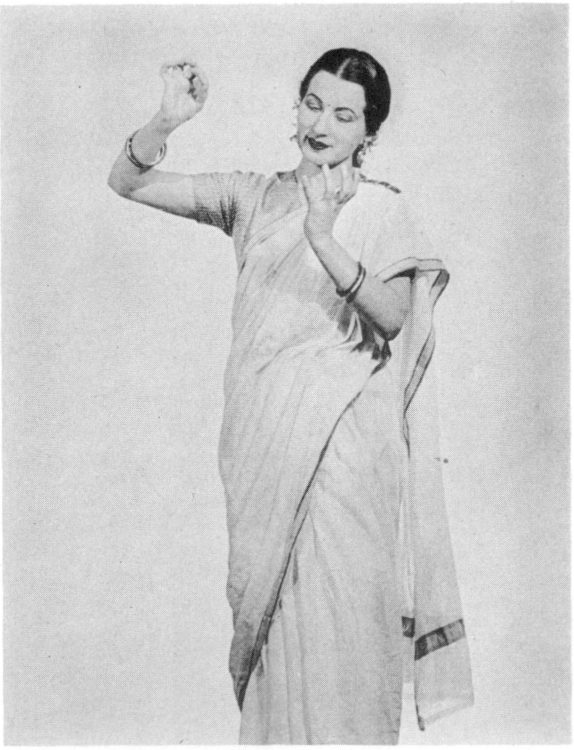

Fig. 32. Bee to Lotus

In Fig. 29 alapadmas in kuñcita show the blooming lotus. (Saṁyuta: udveṣṭitālapadma.) The right hand in Fig. 30 is padmakośa; the left sūcī-mukha. In Fig. 31 the right hand is mukula; the left, patāka. The right hand in Fig. 32 is bhramara and represents the bee which flutters (puṅkhita) above the lotus, which is represented by the left hand in alapadma.

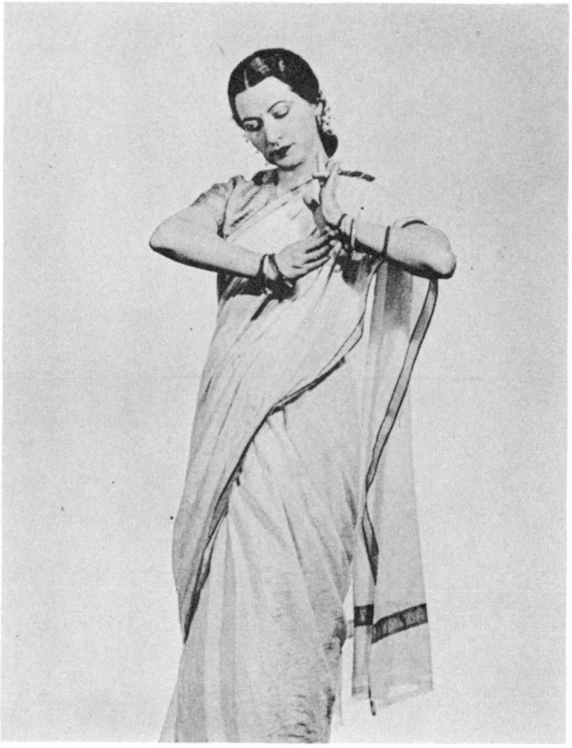

Fig. 33*a*. River

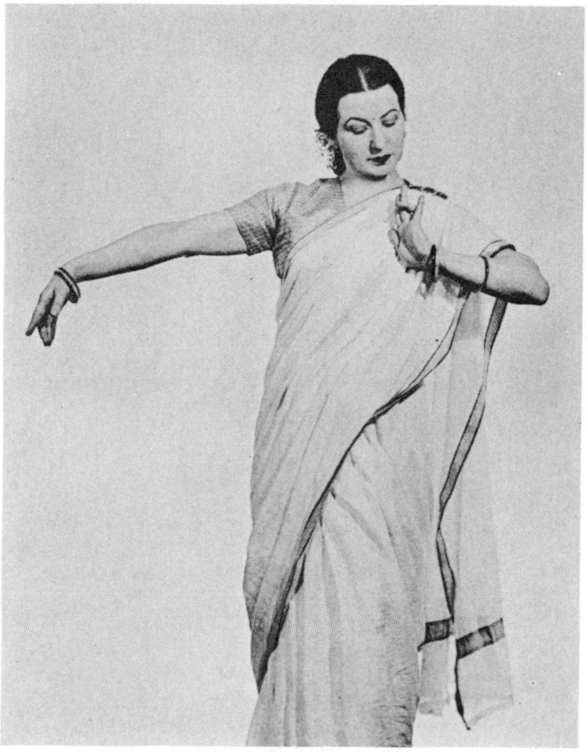

Fig. 33*b*. River

Fig. 34. Waves

Fig. 35. Vines

In Fig. 33*a* the right hand is patāka, the left, tripatāka. The right hand moves in vyāvṛtta, while the arm moves horizontally from left to right. The picture shows the beginning of this movment. Fig. 33*b* shows the end of the movement described in Fig. 33*a*. In Fig. 34 the hands are in patāka. The movement starts with the hands waist high and about a foot apart. From this position they move into the position pictured (prerita) to simulate the rise of the ocean waves. Fig. 35 shows mayūra hasta. The hand revolves on the wrist (recita) so that the extended fingers draw tiny circles. At the same time the arms move from waist height to above the head.

Fig. 36. Rain

Fig. 37. Rain

Fig. 38. Rainbow

Fig. 39. Tempest

In Fig. 36 ūrṇa-nābhas represents light summer rain. For clouds, turn these hands palm upward; for hail, change these hands to lāṅgūlas. In Fig. 37 the left hand is in ūrṇa-nābha, for the cloud; the right, in prasaraṇa of patāka. The right hand, starting from the pose pictured, moves downward in the lines of falling rain. For a torrential downpour, the right hand changes to triśūla. In Fig. 38 the left hand is patāka (for earth); the right, in triśūla, starts from the "earth" and designs the semicircle of the rainbow. In Fig. 39 the left hand in tripatāka remains as pictured. The right, in prasaraṇa of patāka, moves from the pictured position in a long swing downward and backward to shoulder height. At the same time the right hand moves in vyāvṛtta. The movement is quick, heroic, and tumultuous.

Fig. 40. Lightning

Fig. 41. Mountain

Fig. 42. One Day

Fig. 43. Midnight

In Fig. 40 the hand in mayūra designs in the air the sharp zig-zag of lightning. In Fig. 41 the right hand, in alapadma, twists in recita into the position pictured. Fig. 42 shows both hands in tripatāka. The right moves, palm up, under the left and at right angles to it: moves over the left and at right angles with the palm outward; then describes a half-circle into the pictured position. The left hand does not move. The hasta in Fig. 43 is formed in the same way as "one day," save that the right hand tripatāka changes to candra-kalā when it begins the semicircle. Finishing with candra-kalā, as in Fig. 42, means "one night"; finishing as Fig. 43 means midnight. Midday is formed by bringing tripatāka into the position of candra-kalā, as shown in Fig. 43.

Fig. 44. Full Moon Shining on a Water Lily

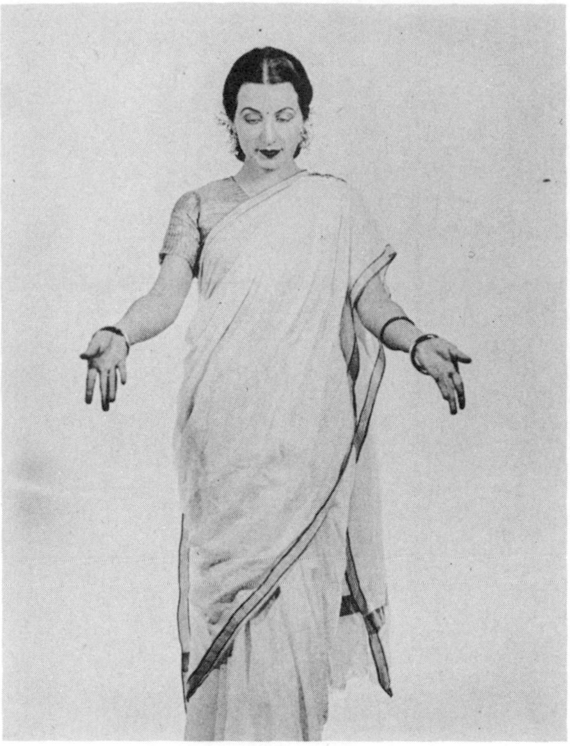

Fig. 45. Flowering Branches

Fig. 46. Flowering Tree

Fig. 47. Mating Season

In Fig. 44 the right hand is alapadma for the full moon; the left, laṅgūla for the water lily. Fig. 45 shows two patākas in prerita. Fig. 46 shows two alapadmas in svastika. Fig. 47 shows tāmra-cūḍas, svastika, indicating mating pigeons.

Fig. 48. Grove of Trees

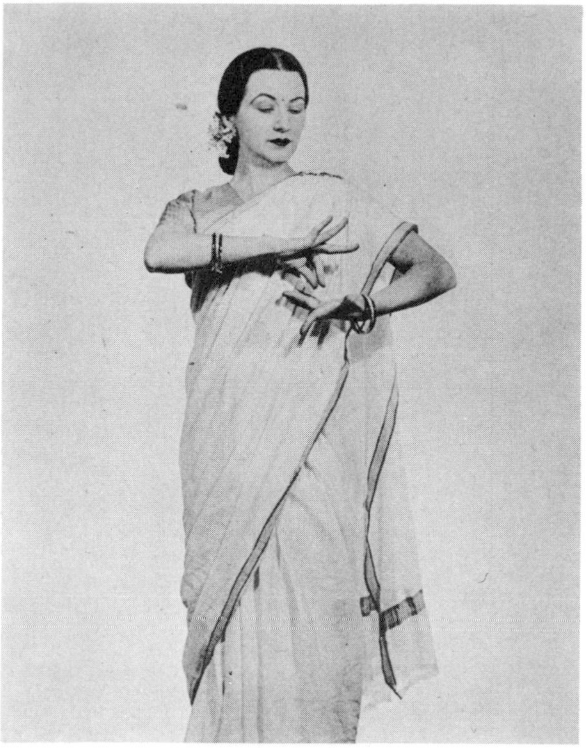

Fig. 49*a*. Anger

Fig. 49*b*. Anger

Fig. 50. Grief

Fig. 48 shows prasaraṇa of ardha-candra, interlaced. (Saṁyuta: karkaṭa.) The hasta in Fig. 49*a* depicts flinging out anger from the heart. The left hand remains in kathakali's ardha-candra (the last three fingers in puṅkhita), while the right changes from the pose pictured (haṁsāsya) to that of the pose in Fig. 49*b*. Fig. 49*b* shows the second phase of the preceding hasta. The right hand is now in alapadma. In Fig. 50 the arms are in śamba; the hands in prasaraṇa of patāka.

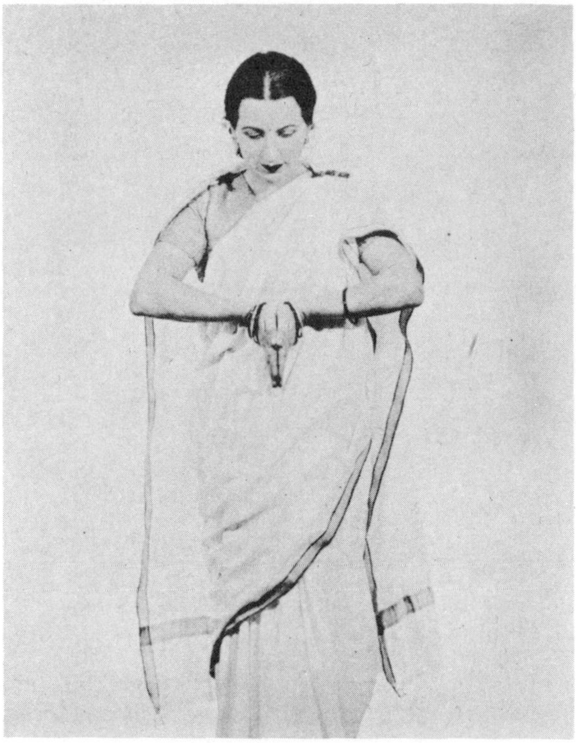

Fig. 51. Sorrow, Weakness

Fig. 52. Seduction

Fig. 53. Revelation

Fig. 54. Sleep

The hands in Fig. 51 are folded patākas, inverted. (Saṁyuta: añjali.) In Fig. 52 the right hand is haṁsāsya; the left arm, gaja. Both hands in Fig. 53 are patāka. The right passes across the forehead. Both hands in Fig. 54 are ardha-candra for patāka.

Fig. 55. Death

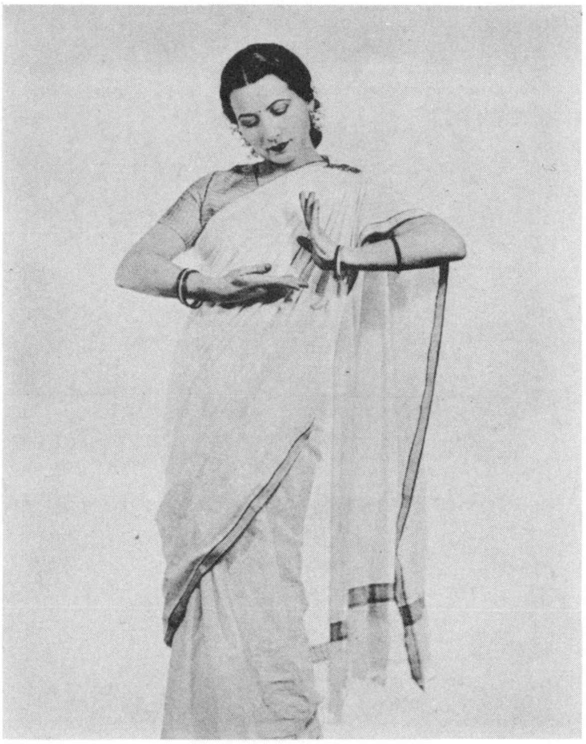

Fig. 56. Perplexity

Fig. 57. Exposition

Fig. 58. Humiliation

Fig. 55 shows sarpa-śīrṣas, folded. (Saṁyuta: kapota.) Both hands in Fig. 56 are patāka and indicate opposing currents in the heart. In 57 the right hand is patāka. In Fig. 58 the hands are prasaraṇa of patāka, in svastika.

Fig. 59. Envy

Fig. 60. Ecstasy

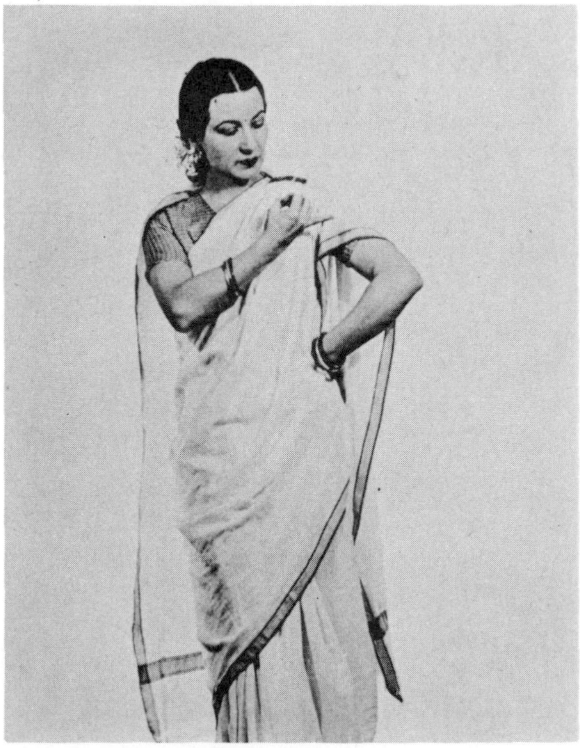

Fig. 61. Disgust

Fig. 62. Intoxication

The right hand in Fig. 59 is śukatuṇḍa; the left, patāka under the heart. The hands in Fig. 60 are moved from the shoulders (as pictured), downward to the hips. (Saṁyuta: nitamba.) The hasta in Fig. 61 is made by closing the hand in bāṇa (as pictured) and then opening it into ardha-candra for patāka. In Fig. 62 the right hand is patāka; the left arm outflung in tola.

Fig. 63. Rest, Meditation

Fig. 64. Meditation

Fig. 65. Laughter

Fig. 66. Torment

In Fig. 63 the right hand is patāka on the breast; the left, candra-kalā at the lips. In Fig. 64 the hand is tripatāka. In Fig. 65 the right hand is prasaraṇa of patāka and half covers the averted face. Patāka hands, upward and downward and over the heart, indicate opposing currents.

Fig. 67. Pity

Fig. 68. Supplication

Fig. 69. Suspicion

Fig. 70. Fear

In Fig. 67 the hands are kaṭaka, interlocked (saṁyuta: kūrma). The palms are twisted against each other to alternate the position of the hands. The folded patākas in fig. 68 make the beautiful salutation of India (above the head, salutation to gods; before the face, to Brahmins; before the chest, to equals). (Saṁyuta: añjali.) Fig. 69 shows alapadmas under the breast. Both hands in Fig. 70 are in arāla and tremble (puṅkhita) violently.

Fig. 71. Fear of a Bee

Fig. 72. Yoga

Fig. 73. Hunger

Fig. 74. Establish

In Fig. 71 the right hand in bhramara (puṅkhita) is the bee; the left (patāka) protects the averted face. In Fig. 72 the right hand in ardha-patāka closes first one nostril and then the other to indicate the measured breathing necessary to the accomplishment of yoga. The hands in Fig. 75 are patāka, svastika on the stomach. This hasta may also indicate food (Saṁyuta: svastika.) The śikhara fist moves firmly downward into the pictured position.

Fig. 75. Amorous

Fig. 76. Passion, Union

Fig. 77. Passion, Union

Fig. 78. Love, Passion

The hands in Fig. 75 are prasarana of patāka, interlocked. The movement is as of stretching and cracking the elbow- and finger-joints. (Saṁyuta: karkaṭa.) In Fig. 76 patāka hands move subtly in bhujaṅga. In Fig. 77 ardha-patākas move in opposite directions, twisting against the pivot of the joined index fingers. In Fig. 78 the hand, in haṁsāsya, describes a tiny circle over the breast.

Fig. 79. Love, Passion

Fig. 80. Two Lovers

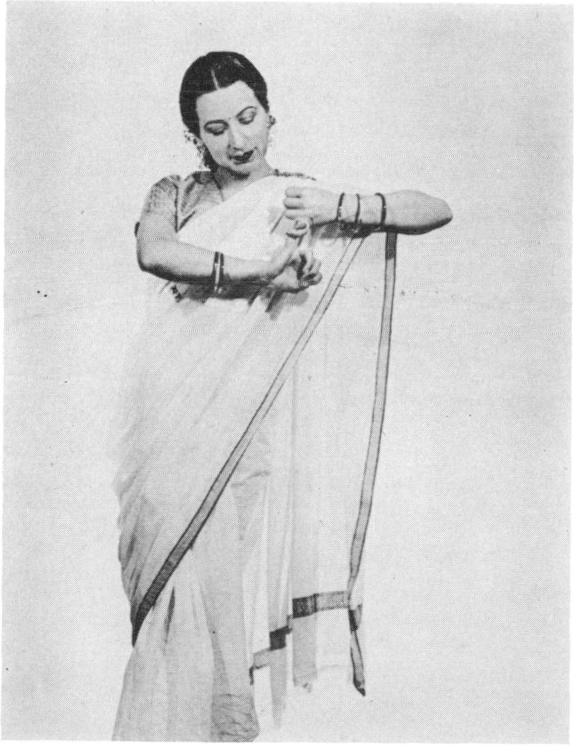

Fig. 81. Friendship

Fig. 82. Marriage

The hand in Fig. 79 is alapadma, puṅkhita. Both hands in Fig. 80 are ardha-sūcika. The hands in Fig. 81 are bāṇa, interlocked. In Fig. 82 the right hand in alapadma resting on the left in ardha-candra indicates the holding of hands in marriage.

Fig. 83. Unrequited Love

Fig. 84. Together

Fig. 85. Lovers' Quarrel

Fig. 86. Together

In Fig. 83 both hands press downward in patāka; the head shakes slightly. The hand in Fig. 84 is ardha-patāka. It can also be used for "we two," "those two," and so forth. The hands in Fig. 85 are ardha-sūcika, interlocked. (Saṁyuta: pāśa.) Used also for "manacles." Both hands are sūcī-mukha.

Fig. 87. Estrangement

Fig. 88. Looking at the Beloved

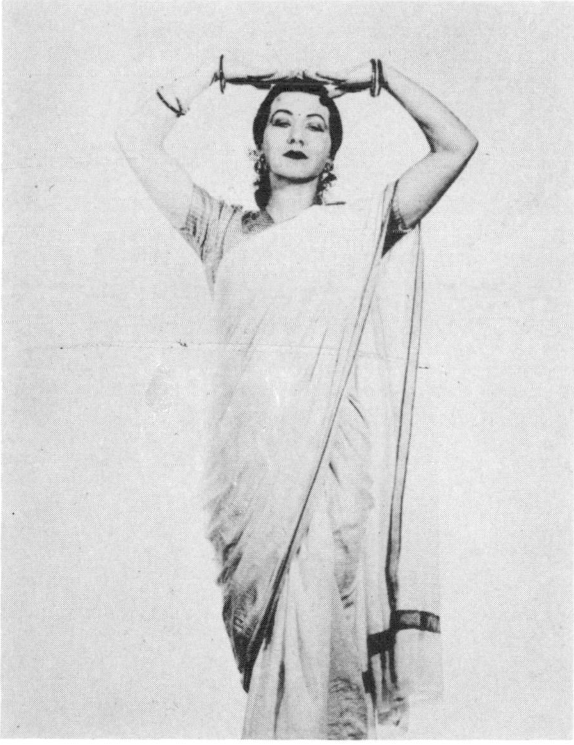

Fig. 89. Beauty of Face

Fig. 90. Loveliness

The hand in Fig. 87 is kartarī-mukha. In Fig. 88 the right hand is apaviddha-sūcī; the left arm, gaja. In Fig. 89 two hands in patāka form a circle around the face from above the forehead, to chest-height. "Beauty of body" can be expressed by a similar circle from chest-height to hip-height. With hands in śikhara as pictured in Fig. 90, the body rocks slightly from the waist. This is the gesture old women make when seeing a lovely young girl.

Fig. 91. Admiration of Feminine Beauty

Fig. 92. Waist

Fig. 93. Lotus-Eyed

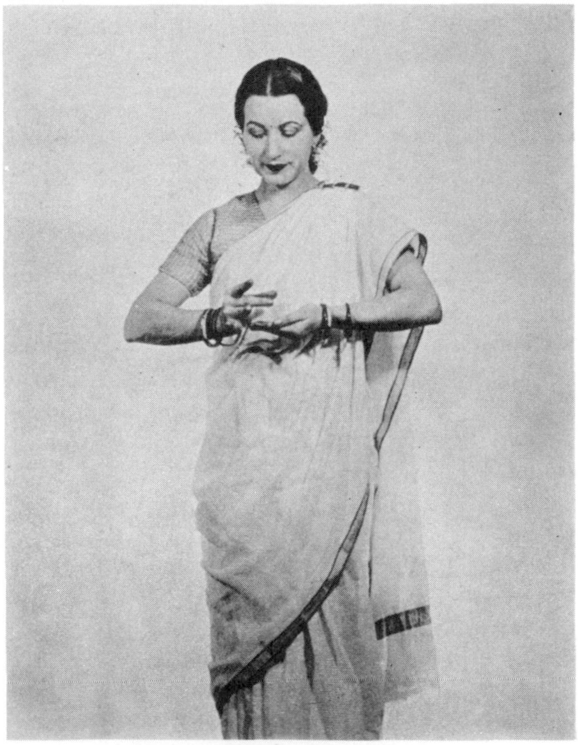

Fig. 94. Sandal-Paste Box

In Fig. 91 the right hand is alapadma; the left, sūcī-mukha. To express "admiration of masculine beauty" change the sūcī to śikhara. In Fig. 92 hands on the waist in ardha-candra indicate "waist." (Saṁyuta: garuḍa-pakṣa.) Then the right hand shows muṣṭi, for "small." The left hand in Fig. 93 is ardha-patāka; the right, alapadma. In Fig. 94 the left hand, in sarpa-śīrṣa, holds the box; the right, in apaviddha-sūcī, unscrews the lid.

Fig. 95. Making Up the Eyebrows

Fig. 96. Comb the Hair

Fig. 97. Putting on Bangles

Fig. 98. Putting on Rings

In Fig. 95 the left hand (sarpa-śīrṣa) holds the box; the right (siṁha-mukha) touches the left palm and then draws the brows as pictured. In Fig. 96 both hands, in ardha-candra, flutter (puṅkhita) downward from the head to the full length of the arm. The same hands turn around each other to form the chignon behind the right ear. They finish with the right in śikhara behind the right ear. (Saṁyuta: keśa-bandha.) In Fig. 97, with the right hand (in apaviddha-sūcī) enclosing the wrist, the left arm turns in recita to the position pictured. For "putting on bracelets" make the same hasta on the upper arm. In Fig. 98 the right hand (apaviddha-sūcī) makes the motions of putting rings on the first three fingers of the left.

Fig. 99. Earring

Fig. 100. Face

Fig. 101. Looking Into A Mirror

Fig. 102. Writing

In Fig. 99 apaviddha-sūcī touches the ear lobe. In Fig. 100 the right hand, in alapadma, starts the movement by spreading beside the right cheek, the thumb under the chin. Pivoting on the thumb, it finishes in the pose pictured. In Fig. 101 the right hand, ardha-candra, is the mirror. Fig. 102 shows the left hand in sarpa-śīrṣa for the board; the right hand (haṁsāsya) moves as though writing.

Fig. 103. Riding

Fig. 104. Grasping

Fig. 105. Holding

Fig. 106. Holding a Necklace

In Fig. 103 the left hand, muṣṭi, holds the reins; the right, candra-kalā, brandishes the whip. The ūrṇa-nābha hand in Fig. 104 closes gently into muṣṭi. The left hand in Fig. 105 is in apaviddha-sūcī. Both hands in Fig. 106 are kaṭakā-mukha, kuñcita.

Fig. 107. Holding a Spear

Fig. 108. Holding Fire

Fig. 109. Holding Garlands

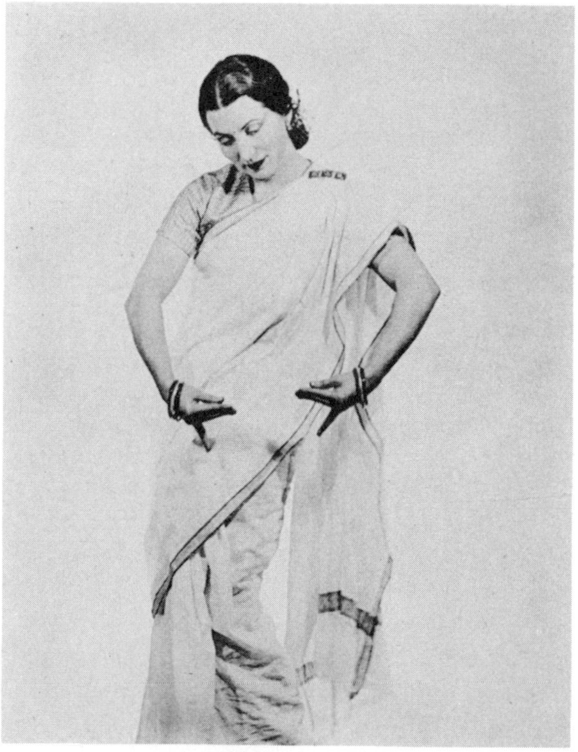

Fig. 110. Gathering Feathers

Both hands in Fig. 107 are mṛga-śīrṣa. The hand in Fig. 108 is opened apaviddha-sūcī. Both hands in Fig. 109 are haṁsāsya. In Fig. 110 haṁsapakṣa hands scoop downward.

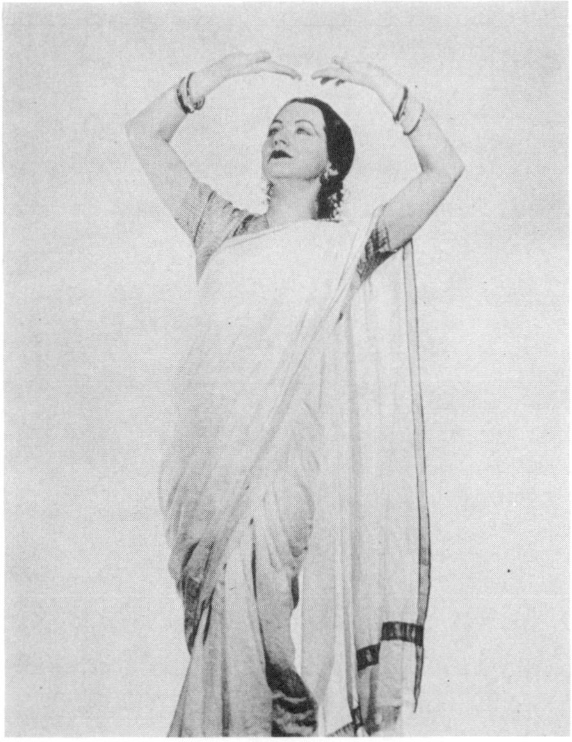

Fig. 111. Shading the Eyes

Fig. 112. Begging

Fig. 113. Sneaking In

Fig. 114. Stroking the Moustache

Both hands in Fig. 111 are patāka in udveṣṭita. The right hand in Fig. 112 is haṁsapakṣa; the left, muṣṭi. In Fig. 113 both hands are in patāka, palms outward (the doors); the left remains in this position while the right passes under it in vyāvṛtta (as pictured). In Fig. 114 the left hand in patāka supports the right elbow. The right hand (kaṭakā-mukha; kuñcita) strokes the upper lip on both sides. Also used for "husband" and "masculine anger."

Fig. 115. Beheading

Fig. 116. Killing

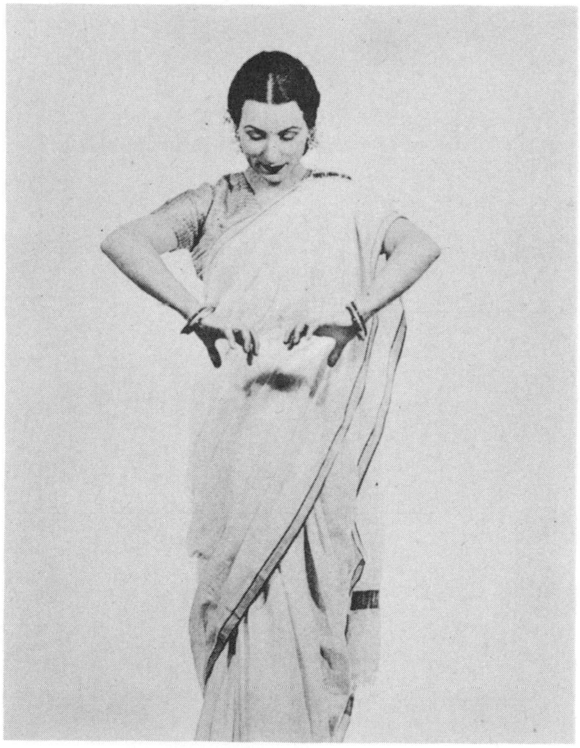

Fig. 117. Disemboweling

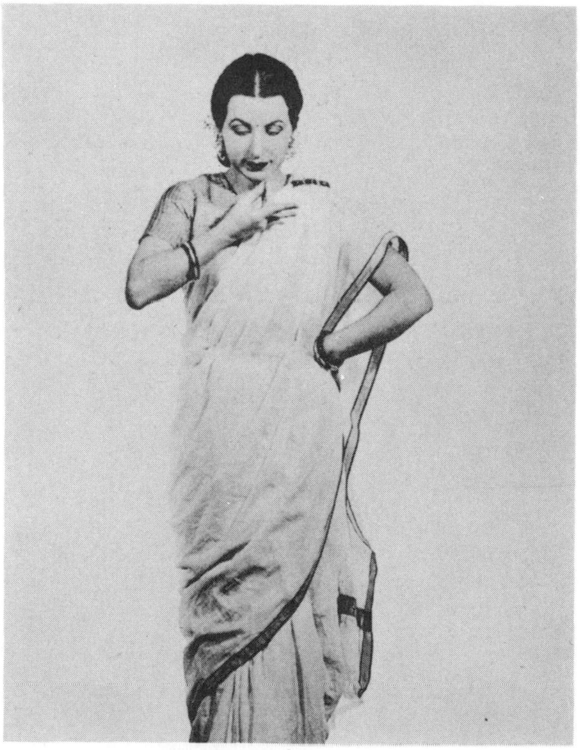

Fig. 118. Smelling

In Fig. 115 the left hand (śikhara) indicates "man." The right (patāka) moves sharply across above the left, from the position as pictured to beyond the śikhara thumb. Fig. 116 is preceded by a definite downward movement of muṣṭi into the position pictured. In Fig. 117, both hands, in ūrṇa-nābha, start close together, then move apart, trembling slightly to suggest force. In Fig. 118 the hand in siṁha-mukha approaches the nose. Also used for "scent," "perfume," and so forth.

Fig. 119. Pulling Out an Arrow

Fig. 120. Drawing a Bow

Fig. 121. Milking Cows

Fig. 122. Driving Cattle

In Fig. 119 the left hand (śikhara) holds the bow; the right (haṁsāsya) pulls an arrow from behind the right shoulder and fits it to the bowstring. Both hands (śikhara) in Fig. 120 make the gesture of drawing a bow. In Fig. 121 both hands (kapittha) make the movement of milking. In Fig. 122 the right hand (sūcī) represents the goad and moves in circles from the wrist. The left (siṁha-mukha) represents the cow and moves in vyāvṛtta. The arms are static.

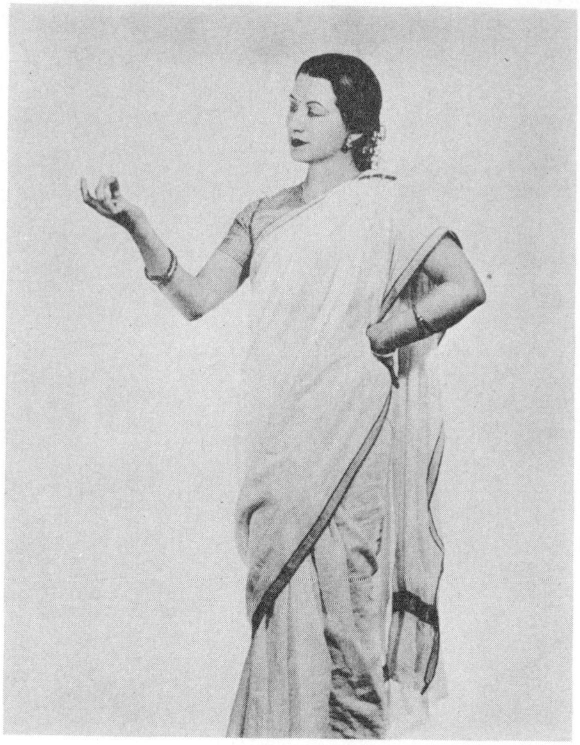

Fig. 123. Beckoning

Fig. 124. Beckoning

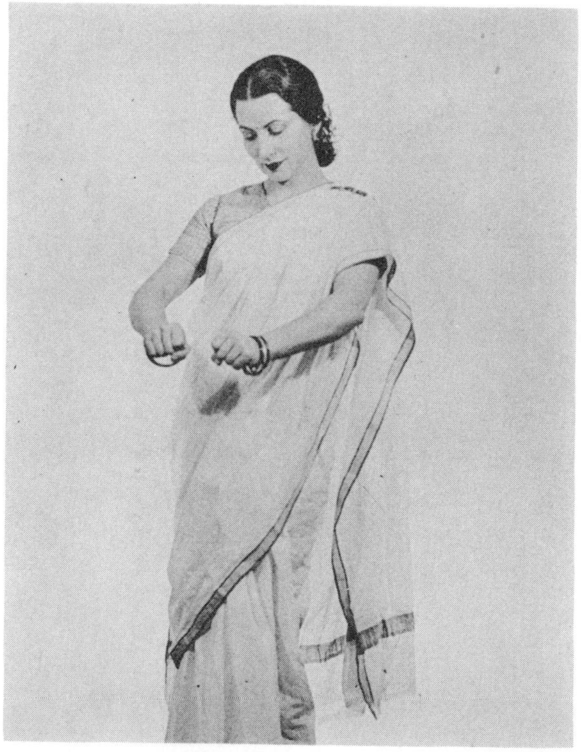

Fig. 125. Breaking

Fig. 126. Breaking a Jar

The hand in Fig. 123 is in apaviddha-sūcī, kuñcita. In Fig. 124 this haṁsapakṣa moves the first three fingers of the hand without separating them. In Fig. 125 both hands, in muṣṭi, bend an object downward. In Fig. 126 both hands, in patāka, outline a jar from bottom to top; then the left hand remains aloft in alapadma, while the right snaps the middle finger against the wrist.

Fig. 127. Showing

Fig. 128. Draping a Sari.

Fig. 129. Refusing

Fig. 130. Refusing

Both hands in Fig. 127 are Kathakali's ardha-candra. In Fig. 128 the right hand (kaṭakā-mukha, kuñcita) moves from the left shoulder over the head to the right shoulder (as pictured) to indicate putting the sari over the head. Both hands in Fig. 129 are patāka. This hasta may also mean "turning away from." When the hands are first closed in bāṇa and then opened as pictured, the hasta means "disgust" (Fig. 61). In Fig. 130 the hand in patāka moves in vyāvṛtta.

Fig. 131. Listening

Fig. 132. Listening

Fig. 133. Listening to Vibrant Sounds (Music)

Fig. 134. Talking

In Fig. 131 two kaṭakā-mukha hands move alternately away from the ear, as though twisting a thread between the thumbs and forefingers and pulling it out at the same time. The right hand in Fig. 132 is in haṁsāsya near the ear. Fig. 133 shows alapadma in puṅkhita. In Fig. 134 the left hand in kaṭakā-mukha near the mouth, opens into candra-kalā, and moves a slight distance away as pictured.

Fig. 135. Talking to a Bird

Fig. 136. Pointing

Fig. 137. Walking

Fig. 138. Walking

In Fig. 135 the right hand (haṁsāsya, puṅkhita) indicates the bird. The left (sūcī-mukha) moves in vyāvṛtta. In Fig. 136 the left hand (patāka) supports the right elbow. Right hand is sūcī-mukha. Both hands in Fig. 137 are patāka. The left follows the right as they move forward in bhujaṅga. In Fig. 138 the fingers pass each other alternately as the hand moves forward in recita of mayūra.

Fig. 139. Walking

Fig. 140. Giving

Fig. 141. Accepting

Fig. 142. Drinking

In Fig. 139 haṁsapakṣa hands move over and in front of each other alternately. The left hand in Fig. 140 is sarpa-śīrṣa; the right touches the left palm in mukula and then assumes the pose pictured. Both hands in Fig. 141 are sarpa-śīrṣa. (Saṁyuta: puṣpapuṭa.) The hasta in Fig. 142 is śikhara.

Fig. 143. Drinking

Fig. 144. Drinking

Fig. 145. Thinking

Fig. 146. Carrying Water (on the Hip)

In Fig. 143 both hands are tripatāka. The right (puṅkhita) moves from the pictured position downward along the throat. The hand in Fig. 144 is sarpa-śīrṣa. In Fig. 145 the left hand (patāka) supports the right elbow. The right hand (candra-kalā in kuñcita) supports the chin. The hands in Fig. 146 are kuñcita of alapadma.

Fig. 147. Carrying Water (on the Head)

Fig. 148. Sprinkling Water

Fig. 149. Watering a Tree

Fig. 150. Washing the Arms

The hands in Fig. 147 are patāka. In Fig. 148 patāka hands, apaveṣṭita, follow the hasta in Fig. 147. The hands in Fig. 149 are alapadma in recita. The hasta suggests emptying a jar of water which is held on the shoulder. In Fig. 150 the left arm is śamba. The right hand, in Kathakali's ardha-candra, scoops up the water from wrist to elbow (as pictured). Then the right hand turns the palm toward the left arm and moves downward to the wrist in puṅkhita to indicate the trickling water.

Fig. 151*a*. Plucking a Flower

Fig. 151*b*. Stringing a Garland

Fig. 152. Scattering Flowers

Fig. 153. Offering a Flower

In Fig. 151*a* tripatāka of the right hand suggests the flower; kaṭakā-mukha of the left plucks it. This hasta should be followed by the one in Fig. 151*b*. In Fig. 151*b* the right hand in kaṭakā-mukha holds the string; the left, in ardha-patāka, loops over it and pulls downward in recita. The left hand (kaṭakā-mukha) in Fig. 152 holds the blossoms; the right (recita of alapadma) drops them to the floor. In Fig. 153 both hands are sūci-mukha, interlaced. The wrists are crossed, and the palms are placed together, with the arms straight down and the finger-tips pointing downward. Then, without unclasping, the hands are turned toward the body and brought upward to the pictured position. This is to represent laying a flower on an altar.

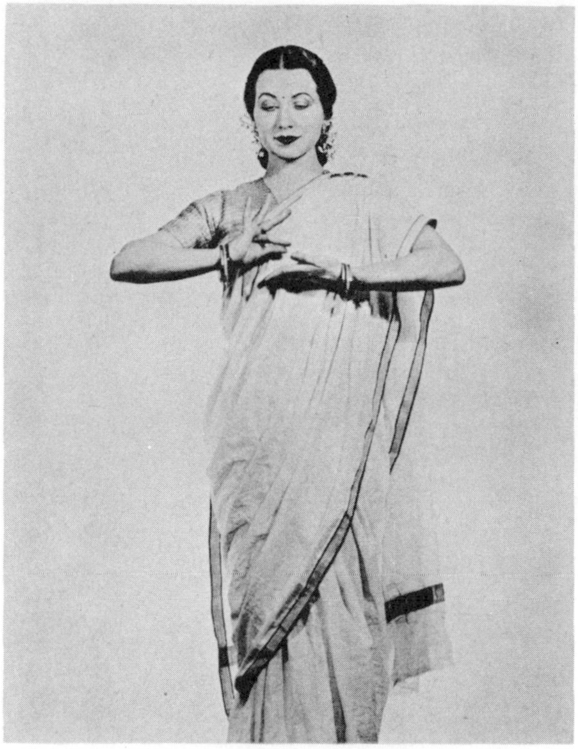

Fig. 154. Flower Spell

Fig. 155. Feeding

Fig. 156. Feeding

Fig. 157. Dance

The left hand in Fig. 154 is patāka; the right, haṁsāsya. In Fig. 155 the left hand, in śikhara, represents the animal fed; the right, mukula, moves in vyāvṛtta. In Fig. 156 sarpa-śīrṣa holds the dish, while mukula offers the food. Both hands in Fig. 157 are siṁha-mukha.

Fig. 158. Dance

Fig. 159. Dance

Fig. 160. Dance

Fig. 161. Music

In Fig. 158 the right forefinger of the apaviddha-sūcī hand touches the cheek. In Fig. 159 the haṁsāsya hand, in kuñcita, grasps the sūcī-mukha hand to frame the face. In Fig. 160 haṁsāsya is on the head. Can also be used to indicate "Pārvatī," creator of the lāsya dance. In Fig. 161 the left hand (mṛga-śīrṣa) and the right (haṁsāsya in vyāvṛtta) suggest the playing of a sitar or vīṇā. This is also used for "rāga."

Fig. 162. Girl

Fig. 163. Gopī

Fig. 164. Old Person

Fig. 165. Warrior

The sarpa-śīrṣa hand in Fig. 162 indicates the height of a young girl. This is also used for "daughter" and "child." In Fig. 163 ardha-patāka hands lift the veil to show the face, then draw it down again. The muṣṭi hand in Fig. 164 suggests the use of a staff. In Fig. 165 the left hand is in muṣṭi for shield; the right in ardha-patāka for sword. This is also used for "fight."

Fig. 166. Prisoner

Fig. 167. Wife

Fig. 168. Beyond

Fig. 169. Dispute

In Fig. 166 haṁsapakṣa hands in svastika indicate bound hands. The hand in Fig. 167 is sūcī-mukha. This can also indicate "woman." In Fig. 168 the right hand, sarpa-śīrṣa in recita, moves from palm down to the pose pictured. Both hands in Fig. 169 are patākas, svastika. The movement points first the finger-tips downward, then as pictured (recita movement).

Fig. 170. Invocation

Fig. 171. Wasting Body

Fig. 172. Evil Eyes

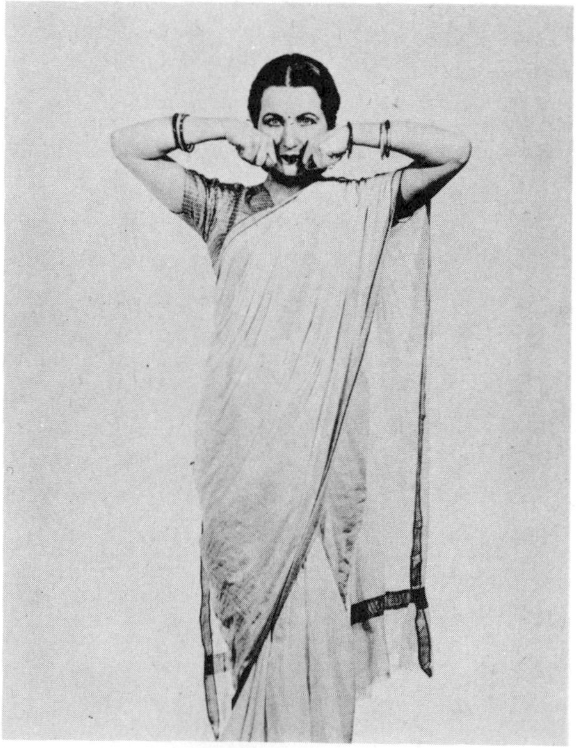

Fig. 173. Fangs

In Fig. 170 both hands are folded patākas above the head. (Saṁyuta: añjali.) The hands in Fig. 171 are śukatuṇḍa, svastika over the heart. In Fig. 172 the hands, in mayūra, kuñcita, beside the eyes, pivot as though twisting a marble between the first fingers and thumbs. The kapittha hands in Fig. 173 indicate fangs. This is used to represent any evil god, goddess, rākṣasa, and so forth.

Fig. 174. I

Fig. 175. You

Fig. 176. "Go Away!"

Fig. 177. "What Shall I Do?"

In Fig. 174 ardha-candra is for patāka. Fig 175 is patāka. The arm in Fig. 176 is tola. The hand is prasaraṇa of patāka. The entire movement is away from. In sūcī-mukha the right hand in Fig. 177 moves from left to right before the face.

Fig. 178. "What Shall I Do?"

Fig. 179. "What Happens?"

Fig. 180. "Come Here!"

Fig. 181. "All of Us"

The left hand in Fig. 178 is śikhara; the right patāka. In Fig. 179 the right hand in śikhara moves from the left shoulder to the pictured position. The right hand (kaṭakā-mukha) in Fig. 180 grasps the left wrist and moves the left arm from an extension straight in front of the body into the gaja pose pictured. This may also be used for "I took him there" or "I will take you there." In Fig. 181 the hands in patāka move from straight in front, waist-height, to directly out at the side. The picture is taken about half-way through this movement. This may also represent "all of you" or "everyone."

Fig. 182. "Listen to Me!"
(in an angry tone)

Fig. 183. "Come here!"

Fig. 184. Siva

Fig. 185. Siva

Fig. 182 is candra-kalā, vyāvṛtta. The hand in Fig. 183 is patāka and should be preceded by the pose in Fig. 175. Fig. 184 shows one of the many hastas for Śiva. Here he is described as "the three-eyed god." The right hand moves three fingers (triśūla); the left passes across the brow and eyes. In Fig. 185 Śiva is "cobra-crowned." The left hand, sūcī-mukha, points to the crown; the right, sarpaśīrṣa, indicates the cobra.

Fig. 186. Siva

Fig. 187. Siva

Fig. 188. Siva

Fig. 189. Viṣṇu

Fig. 186 shows Śiva as "he who wears the moon in his hair." The right hand, candra-kalā, represents the moon; the left, alapadma, the crown. In Fig. 187 Śiva is "the god who rides the bull." The left hand, in siṁha-mukha, represents the bull. The right, in śikhara, represents man. Any god may be named by using a śikhara atop the hasta for that god's favorite mount (see Fig. 200). In Fig. 188 Śiva is "the creator of the earth and heavens." Two patāka hands moving in opposite directions indicate the heavens and the earth; or, both hands udveṣṭita (earth), then both apaveṣṭita (heavens). Viṣṇu is indicated, as in Fig. 189, by kaṭakā-mukha hands.

Fig. 190. Viṣṇu Devotee

Fig. 191. Blessings of the Gods

Fig. 192. Hanuman (the Monkey-God)

Fig. 193. Kṛṣṇa

In Fig. 190 patāka hand at the thigh indicates that "the ocean of mundanity is thigh-deep to Viṣṇu devotees." The hands in Fig. 191 are alapadma in recita prāṇa. Also used for "Heaven." Both hands in Fig. 192 are patākas on gaja and apaviddha arms. In Fig. 193 hands in bāṇa indicate the flute of Kṛṣṇa.

Fig. 194*a*. Kṛṣṇa and Rādhā

Fig. 194*b*. Kṛṣṇa and Rādhā

Fig. 195. Kṛṣṇa

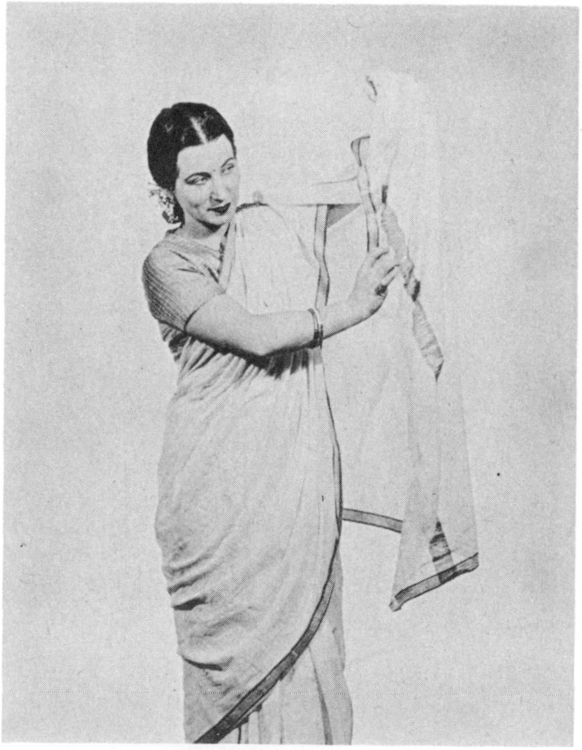

Fig. 196. Peeping at Kṛṣṇa

In Fig. 194*a* the left hand (ūrṇa-nābha) is Rādhā; the right (bāṇa) Kṛṣṇa, who grasps her to pull her toward him. In Fig. 194*b* the left hand (in muṣṭi) is Kṛṣṇa, and the right (patāka) is Rādhā, who demurs at the ardor of the Divine Lover. This movement and the one in Fig. 194*a* are alternated. In Fig. 195 Kṛṣṇa is indicated by Kaṭakā-mukha hands. This gesture is also used for Viṣṇu, since Kṛṣṇa is an avatār of Viṣṇu. In Fig. 196, the left hand in inverted patāka, holds the sari, while the right (apaviddha) draws it coyly aside.

Fig. 197. Rāvaṇa

Fig. 198. Goddess

Fig. 199. Kāma-Dahana

Fig. 200. Indra

Rāvaṇa, having ten heads, the right hand in sūcī-mukha, as in Fig. 197, points ten times across the forehead in vyāvṛtta prāṇa. In Fig. 198 the iconografic mudrā of protection (patāka pointed up) and bestowal (patāka pointed down) indicate a goddess. Identification of the goddess is supplied by indicating her spouse. (Example, "Pārvatī" shown by using Fig. 198 followed by Fig. 187). Fig. 199 shows the God of Love. As with us, Cupid is an archer. The left hand, śikhara, and the right, kaṭakā-mukha, indicate his delicate weapon. In Fig. 200 the left hand (bāṇa, elephant) and the right (śikhara) indicate the god who rides the elephant.

GLOSSARY

GLOSSARY

Abhinaya: the suggestive imitation of moods and emotions of play characters; rhythmic showing.

Āchārya: dancing master.

Achkan: coat worn by the male Kathak dancers. Its full circular skirt falls from the waist to the ankles (Moghul type).

Addiyaṃ: neck movement; also called "grīvā rechaka." Most characteristic are the sundari (horizontal movements of the head on the neck) and prakampita (like a pigeon).

Aṇgikābhinaya: bodily pantomime; rhythmic bodily expository movements; movements of body and legs.

Añjali: invocational saṁyuta; see Fig. 170.

Apsaras: celestial nymph.

Asaṁyuta: single-handed poses.

Aucitya: appropriateness to time, place, idea, the form of art, and the nature of the individual concerned.

Avatār: incarnation or "descent" of a god.

Banya: one of a pair of drums called "tablas." The banya is the left-hand drum. It is made of a sort of copper pot with a drumhead pulled over the top and tuned by blocks run through the strings which hold the skin on. A mixture of flour and water and iron filings is rubbed into the off-center of the drumhead. This is called the āk (eye). It gives a highly resonant tone to that part of the drumhead. The left hand may strike the banya on the ak, the warka (skin between ak and kanar), or the kanar (the rim of heavier skin which holds the skin onto the drum). Besides, each of these three may be struck with separate fingers, with the whole hand, and also with resonant or muffled sound. The banya is held in the hollow of the bent knees when the drummer sits cross-legged on the floor.

Bhagavad Gītā: "Song of the Blessed One." A poem included in the Mahābhārata. "This is a philosophical poem, possessing moreover brilliantly poetical qualities."

Bhāgavata Purāṇa: a book telling the powers and works of Hindu gods; *see also* Puraṇa.

Bharata: a sage; authority on Nāṭya and author of the Nāṭya Sāstra.

Bharata Nāṭya: the art of Nāṭya (dance and drama combined); the classical dance-form of India.

Bharata Nāṭyam: the classical lāsya dance-form, whose center is in Madras.

Bhāva: emotion; mood—the psychological state which precedes rasa-realization.

Bhāvanī: a name given to the feminine principle or śakti.

Bola: a phrase or sentence of rhythmic syllables used in Kathak dancing. Example:

"Ta ta ta tuk
Dun nuna gita kita
Toh toranga taka
Tun taka dada gina
Tay . . . taka
Tun taka dada gina
Tay . . . taka
Tun taka dada gina
Ta tay tat tay
Ta tay tat tay
Tay ta tey ta tay
Te te tat tat
Tah."

There are four beats to each line of the example herewith given.

Brahmānanda: oneness with God; yoga-union.

Chidambaram: the mythical fields on which Śiva danced and where Kṛishṇa dallied with the gopīs; the scene of the Gīta Govinda; the heart of the devotee; sometimes called "Tillai."

Daina: the right-hand drum of the pair called "tabla." The daina is cylindrical, slightly conic, and of wood, with the ak placed in the center of the drumhead; otherwise it is identical with the banya (*see* Banya). It is rested on the floor to the right of the tabla player.

Dévas: gods. Generally applied to any gods of lesser importance than the Trimūrti of Brahmā, Śiva, Vishṇu; secondary gods; celestials.

Dharma: law, or right conduct. Kāma (enjoyment), artha (acquisition,) and dharma (righteousness) make trivarga (perfect blending of ethics).

Dōmbaka, *see* Śilpaka.

Drone: the long, steady note which sustains all Indian music. It may "be a drum, carefully tuned, or two drums, in unison or at an octave, or the drone strings of the veena; but is as a rule . . . a tambura, a large veena-shaped instrument, with one gourd (sound-board) instead of two—and with open strings . . ." (from *The Music of Hindustan*, by Fox-Strangeways). The word "drone" is often applied to the instrument upon which it is played.

Esraj: an instrument with metal frets and seventeen strings. It is held vertically and bowed somewhat like a cello.

Gandharva: a musical inhabitant of Indra's paradise. The Gandharvas espoused the Apsaras. The term is sometimes used to mean aesthetic public as against the royal house and the sacradotal class.

Gargari: the gored skirt worn by Marwari women and female Kathak dancers, measuring from twenty to two hundred yards around the bottom.

Gaths: pantomimic passages in North Indian dancing; *see* p. 17.

Gīta Govinda: lyric poem by Jaidev, a Bengali poet between the 12th and the 13th centuries, recounting the adventures of Kṛishṇa and Rādhā and the gopīkas on the fields of Chidambaram.

Gopī (gopikā): milkmaid.

Gopuram: the tower over the gates which give access to a Hindu temple; characteristic of Carnatic architecture.

Guru: teacher.

Hasta: hand.

Hastābhinaya: hand-pantomime.

Hasta-prāṇa: life-force of a hand; loosely, hand movement.

Jhaptal: sometimes called "zhapa" or "jhampa tala." It has ten mātrās; scans as two long feet and one short. Each āvard has one sama and two vibhāgs. It can be counted as 10–8 time.

Kalasam: Incidental dance (Kathakali)

Karaṇas: "a karaṇa in dance is the co-ordination of the movements of the hand and foot." Bharata, Nāṭya Sāstra (Verse 30).

Kathak: a form of North Indian dance: see p. 16.

Kathakali: a form of South Indian dance-drama; see p. 11. The title is not Sanskrit, but Malayallam.

Kiṅkiṇī: dancing bells of silver, brass, or copper. They are strung "on blue cords" with a knot between each bell. There are worn one hundred or more on each ankle. Sometimes called "gajjai."

Kṛṣṇa: a hero deified into an avatar of Vishnu. The classic spelling "Kṛṣṇa" has been used in the description of the mudrās for scholars of Sanskrit. The more usual phonetic spelling of "Kṛishṇa" has been used in the text for greater facility in reading.

Kṛishṇa-gopāla, Kṛishṇa the Cowherd, is a favorite in Indian art, where he is often represented as playing the flute.

Lāsya: lyric feminine dance originated by Pārvatī.

Lokadharma: imitative realism; natural action; world ways.

Mahābhārata: an epic poem of the great Bharata nation. It recounts a great war in which all the warlike races of Northern India took part, supposedly in the 13th or the 14th century B.C. With the passage of the centuries this much beloved poem has been added to until the whole is now composed of eighty-five thousand couplets.

Mahāgītā: gesture-song.

Manipuri: a form of Northeast Indian dance. See p. 19.

Mantra, or mantram: pantomimed religious chant. The Mantrapāṭha is the prayer book of the Āpastambins and contains 590 mantras to be recited at domestic rites and ceremonials.

Mṛgaśīrṣa: April

Mohinī-attam: "attam" means "rhythm." Kṛishṇa-attam is the perfect example of pure Sanskrit drama. Mohinī-attam is so called because the feminine role is named Mohinī.

Moods, *see* Rasas.

Moṭitam: knees spread wide, and bent until the thighs are horizontal with the floor.

Mudrā: Iconographic term for hand-pose.

Mukhaja: facial mime; technique of the facial muscles toward stylized pantomime.

Muni: sage.

Naṭa: dancer.

Naṭa sūtra: exposition of dancing written in the poetic form known as "sūtra." Its authors were Śilāli and Kṛśāśva.

Nāṭya: combination of dance and drama. In the oriental theater these two can never be completely divorced.

Nāṭyadharma: imaginative transfiguration; stylized action; stage ways.

Nāṭya Śāstra: Bharata's book setting forth the rules of the stage and the technique of the dance and the drama. See p. 10. Written in śloka form. "Śāstra" means "science"; "nāṭya," "dance."

Nautch: a combination of dance, song, and music. See p. 15.

Nṛtta: pure dance; dance without specific meaning.

Nṛtya: pantomimic dance; dance without song, which nevertheless tells a story.

Purāṇas: Holy Books. There are two groups of Purāṇas—the Mahā Purāṇas and the Upa Purāṇas. The Mahā Purāṇas, which are the most important, deal with the creation of the universe, the cycles of mankind and such subjects. The Upa Purāṇas are sectarian in character, and of a purely local interest. There are eighteen Mahā Purāṇas, and their titles are as follows: Viṣṇu Purāṇa, Garuḍa Purāṇa, Bhāgavata Purāṇa, Brahmavaivarta Purāṇa, Bhaviṣyat Purāṇa, Matsya Purāṇa, Vāyu Purāṇa, Agni Purāṇa, Saṁhita Purāṇa, Padma Purāṇa, Harivaṁśa Purāṇa, Mārkaṇḍeya Purāṇa, Brahma Purāṇa, Linga Purāṇa, Kūrma Purāṇa, and Devībhāgavatam Purāṇa.

Rāga: melodic mold.

Rāmāyaṇa: an epic poem setting forth the adventures of the pure hero Rāma and his wife, Sītā, and brother Lakṣṣmaṇa. Originally the work of Vālmīki about a thousand years before Christ, it has been added to until now it is composed of seven books (500 cantos and 24,000 couplets in śloka meter).

Rasa: mood; flavor; aesthetic emotion in the philosophic sense. The Love of God is rasa.

Rasas, The Nine: *See* p. 12.

Rasa-realization: the realization, or attainment, of feeling rasa.

Rasavant: rasa-full. Possessed of rasa.

Sādhakas: students of the law, Saddharma.

Sadir Nautch: combination of gesture-song and dance. *See* p. 15.

Śaivic: pertaining to Śiva.

Samgīta: combination of gīta (song), nṛtya (mime), and vādya (instrumental music).

Saṁyuta: combined hand-pose.

Śāstra: science.

Sāttvika abhinaya: the eight sattvika bhāvas —stambha (fixity); svēda (sweating); romāñca (horripilation); svarabheda (change of voice); vepathū (trembling); vaivarṇya (blushing); aśru (shedding tears); pralaya (fainting).

Serangi: an instrument, stringed and bowed. Larger than the esraj, and more uncommon. Three large gut strings are bowed, while an infinite number of wire strings vibrate in harmony as the drone.

Śilpaka: Śilpaka and Dombaka are types of

very vulgar dramatic representation including the black art and other despised practices in their themes.

Śūdras: non-Aryans. In the second millenium B.C. Aryas (Sanskrit) from Iran wrested India from the Dravidians (Deccan). To preserve the purity of their race they created a social gulf between themselves and the non-Aryans (Śūdras) by establishing three classes of society among themselves. Today these four are the main castes of India: The philosophers and educators (Brahmins); the administrators and soldiers (Kshattriyas); the tradesmen and farmers (Vaiśśyas); and the craftsmen and laborers (Śūdras).

Sūtra: a poetic treatise; an expository composition in meter.

Sūtradhāra: stage manager; producer.

Tablas: pair of drums; the daina and the banya.

Tāl: tāla.

Tāla: the rhythmic design of Hindu music. *See* p. 17.

Tāṇḍava: one of Śiva's gaṇas (attendants).

Tāntrik: the Tantras are rituals which deal with the power of serpent, yoga, esoteric knowledge, and so forth.

Thattadavu: *see* p. 15.

Torahs: rhythmic sequences of the Kathak school of dance. *See* p. 17.

Trimūrti: trinity of Brahmā, Vishṇu, and Śiva.

Tripatāka: an asaṁyuta; *see* Fig. 4.

Upanishads: books written some thousand years before Christ by the Kosalas of Oudh and the Videhas of North Behar, containing researches into the mysteries of the soul and into the nature of the One Universal Soul which pervades the creation—the metaphysical Absolute; philosophic-religious meditations appended to the sacred text of the Vedas.

Upavishṭa sthānaka: sitting on the heels, with the knees spread wide and the weight on the half-toes.

Vartanas: arm carriage; the position of the arm in space.

Veda: religious scriptures; rules of a creed. The Vedas were orally handed down until the 6th century. The Kosalas and Videhas compiled the Vedic hymns. The Brāhmaṇas were commentaries on the Vedas, as were the Upanishads which they preceded. "The Veda is eternal, the sacred books its temporal expression." Each Veda is a science of human expression which proceeds from and returns to God.

Vedânta: the theory of the Vedas. The Vedânta are inquiries into philosophy. They are "the first system of true philosophy which the world has produced."

Vijayanagar: The vijayanager kingdom lasted from 1358 to 1565. Its territory was approximately that of the Madras Presidency today. The course of this empire saw the rule of ten monarchs before it was finally crushed by the Moslem States.

Viniyoga: meaning; the application of certain poses to convey certain ideas.

Viṣṇavite: pertaining to Vishṇu.

Viṣṇu: Vishṇu. The classic spelling of "Viṣṇu" has been used in the description of the mudras for scholars of Sanskrit. The more usual phonetic spelling of "Vishṇu" has been used in the test for greater facility in reading.

Vyāvṛtta: a hasta-prāṇa (*see* pp. 29).

Yoga-union: mental concentration to attain a certain end.

THE VINIYOGA OF THE HASTA MUDRĀS

[Except when otherwise indicated, the numbers refer to figure numbers

Intoxication, 62
Invocation, 170

Jackal, 5
Jar, 126

Kāma-dahana, 199; mukula asaṁyuta, p. 31
Kill, 116; śikhara asaṁyuta, p. 33
Krishna, 193, 194, 195, 196

Laksmī, kapittha asaṁyuta, p. 35
Laughter, 65
Leaves, ardha-patāka asaṁyuta, p. 30
Lightening, 40
Light offering, arāla asaṁyuta, p. 33
Listen, 131, 132, 133, 182; sūcī-mukha, p. 31; haṁsāsya, p. 36, saṁdaṁśa, p. 37 (asaṁyutas)
Look, 88, 196
Lotus, 29, 30, 32, 44
Lotus bud, 31
Lotus eyed, 93
Love, 47, 78, 79, 83, 199; *see also* Amorous, Passion, Union
Loveliness, 90
Lovers, 80, 88; *see also* Together
Lovers' quarrel, 85; *see also* Dispute, Estrangement

Man, 187
Marriage, 82
Mating season, 47
Me, 174
Measure, candra-kalā asaṁyuta, p. 31
Meditation, 63, 64; *see also* Yoga
Midnight, 43
Milk cows, 121
Milkmaid, 121, 163
Mirror, 101
Monkey-god, 192
Month, patāka asaṁyuta, p. 30
Moon, 44, 186
Mountain, 41
Moustache, 114
Music, 133, 161

Nandi (the Bull of Śiva), 187
Necklace, 100
Night, 42, 43
No, haṁsāsya asaṁyuta, p. 36
Nose, sūcī-mukha asaṁyuta, p. 31

Ocean, *see* Water, Waves
Odor, 118
Offer, 140, 153, 156; kapittha asaṁyuta, p. 35
Old person, 164

Painting eyebrows, 95
Palace, alapadma asaṁyuta, p. 33
Parrot, śuka-tuṇḍa asaṁyuta, p. 34
Partridge, lāṅgūla asaṁyuta, p. 36
Passion, 76, 77; *see also* Love, Seduction, Union
Past, patāka asaṁyuta, p. 30
Peacock, 8, 9, 11; mayūra asaṁyuta, p. 36
Peep, 196
Perfume, 118
Perplexity, 56, 177, 178, 179
Pigeons, 47
Pity, 67
Plate, ardha-candra asaṁyuta, p. 31
Play (a musical instrument), 161
Pluck, 151*a*
Point, 136; sūcī-mukha asaṁyuta, p. 31
Prisoner, 166
Pull, 119, 151*a*; śuka-tuṇḍa asaṁyuta, p. 34

Quarrel, 85; *see also* Dispute, Estrangement

Rādhā, 174*a* and *b*
Rāga, 161
Rain, 36, 37; ūrṇa-nābha asaṁyuta, p. 37 (of flowers) padmakośa asaṁyuta, p. 32
Rainbow, 38
Rāvana, 197
Refuse, 129, 130, 176
Rest, 63
Return, tripatāka asaṁyuta, p. 30
Revelation, 53
Ride, 103
Rings, put on, 98
River, 33*a* and *b*
River bank, ardha-patāka asaṁyuta, p. 30
Run, patāka asaṁyuta, p. 30

Salvation, siṁha-mukha asaṁyuta, p. 32
Sarasvatī, kapittha asaṁyuta, p. 35
Sari, 128
Scatter, 152; catura asaṁyuta, p. 35